A Walk Through the Gardens with God

God's Plan to Bring You Home to Heaven

Carl Floyd

Copyright © 2025 Carl Floyd
All rights reserved.
ISBN: 979-8-9925375-2-9
Library of Congress Number: 2025902406

Ross Creek Publishing

(All Scripture reference are RSV-CE unless otherwise noted)

DEDICATION

To my wonderful wife, Catherine without whom I would have never come home to the Catholic Church. Without whom I would never have ventured to undertake such a work. With patience and love, you have been a constant encouragement to me. Always and forever, I love you!

CONTENTS

Prologue

Opening the Garden Gate

If you long for a mind at rest and a heart that cannot harden, go find a gate that opens into a garden! (Helen Hayes)

There is something special about gardens. It doesn't really matter if it's a vegetable garden, a Japanese friendship garden, a formal rose garden, or just a country flower garden. I am drawn to the memories of helping grandma pick hollyhocks, tomatoes, green beans, and all sorts of flowers and vegetables. The heavy fragrance of the hybrid roses in the evening air, a cool breeze gently stirring, the full flavor of a warm tomato eaten from the vine; these are memories of those lazy summer evenings in grandma's garden. Gardens can be such wonderful places!

Scripture tells of four significant gardens that frame our journey of faith in this world and the world to come. We find the beginning and completion of the human experience in these four gardens. We encounter the challenges and sacrifices, the losses and the victories of life and death. In these gardens, we find the Almighty who seeks to be our Friend, our Father, and our God.

As we stroll through these gardens together, we will encounter the beauty and wonder of perfect happiness and complete fulfillment in the Garden of Eden. Sadly, we will witness the loss of God's friendship for all humankind. We will grapple with the aftermath of that loss. The struggles, sufferings, physical and spiritual battles resulting from sin; humanity's prideful rebellion against God. In the Garden of Gethsemane, we will witness the culmination of this struggle and gain insight into how we can also overcome the world. In the Garden of Resurrection, we will encounter the risen Savior and hear him call us by name. We will be renewed in our hope of peace with God in this garden. Finally, in the Garden of Paradise, we will enter the perfect place of life and peace that God has intended for us since the beginning. We will experience all things made new.

I know you are thinking, "if only it were that simple, that easy!" Our experience in life tells us that gardening is hard work. The sun beats down, threatening to destroy the tender shoots of growth. Watering the garden is an ongoing balancing act; not enough water, everything shrivels and dies, too much, and it all drowns. And let's not even talk about weeding! Something seems entirely upside down when the weeds outgrow and choke off the good that has been planted. Tending a garden is time-consuming. Tending a garden requires backache-inducing labor. It is so much easier to go to the local grocery store produce aisle. Quick, convenient satisfaction! Yet few pleasures compare with enjoying a harvest from one's own garden!

Unfortunately, we want that same quick, convenient satisfaction when it comes to the garden of our lives. Scripture is replete with references to planting and tending and watering, and in St. Paul's words, a harvest "in due season" (Gal. 6:9). In that same passage, we are encouraged to "not lose heart." In other words, it has always been difficult. There have been no shortcuts from the time Adam heard God declare that it would be, "by the sweat of your brow" that the garden would produce its life-sustaining bounty.

One summer, my family visited my grandmother. In her frailty, she struggled with the upkeep of her vegetable garden. The weeds were threatening to overrun the garden. The harvest was in danger of being lost. Grandma asked my brothers and me to spend a bit of time pulling weeds for her. I am embarrassed to report that we all hemmed and hawed and found other ways to spend that summer afternoon. We returned from our distractions to find a couple of the neighbor's kids pulling weeds. We didn't mind too much. After all, we were visiting and having fun. Then, when the weeds were pulled and the work done, grandma pulled out her purse and paid those who had worked in the garden. Suddenly, the day's revelry lost a bit of its luster. And the look of hurt on grandma's face as she turned back towards us and simply said, "I would have paid you boys." Ouch! We had lost so much more than a few measly dollars.

In this journey of faith, we have the opportunity to turn away from the work of the garden. The distractions of life, the pleasures of the world around us, and the seemingly urgent responsibilities all cry out for our attention. And amidst the clamor of competing priorities, it is very easy to let the gentle wooing of the garden be put off to a more convenient time. Yet, somehow, that time seldom comes. There is always a more critical demand, a more pressing matter. The day will come, and we will look at the harvest of our lives and wonder where it all went, what difference did it all make? Or was the writer of Ecclesiastes right, "all is vanity and striving after wind" (Eccl. 1:14). Certainly, there must be more than just the hectic race that passes as life.

In the next few chapters, we will look at four gardens found in Scripture. As we learn about these gardens, we will gain insights into our journey of faith in this life and the life to come - where we started, where God wants us to go, and what we encounter along the way.

Chapter 1

God's Garden of Perfect Unity and Peace

Genesis 2:8 And the Lord God planted a garden in Eden, in the east; and there he put the man whom he had formed.

Genesis 2:10: A river flowed out of Eden to water the garden, and there it divided and became four rivers.

Genesis 2:18: Then the Lord God said, "It is not good that the man should be alone; I will make him a helper fit for him."

God planted a garden. Not just any garden, but the garden of Eden. As we read the description of this garden, we quickly realize it is unlike any garden on earth. Imagine the most spectacular landscape ever. In fact, it is *paradesio!* An idyllic place where four rivers flow bringing the waters of life from the garden, their gentle burbling accompanying the breezes that rustle the leaves and branches. The sweet song of birds rises to tickle the ears.

And the trees! Majestic trees with branches spread out to provide shade, shelter, and sustenance. "Every tree that was delightful to look at and good for food, with the tree of life in the middle of the garden and the tree of the knowledge of good and evil" (Gen. 2:9). The intoxicating fragrance of blossoms floats on the gentle breezes. Winding paths cross a meadow filled with sheep fearlessly frolicking with wolves. There is no discord, no bickering. There is no pain or suffering in this garden. There is no separation, no death.

This garden is an incredibly special place indeed. It is a place of abundance, a place of peace. It is the divine intersection of Heaven and earth. It is most incredible because it is here, in the Garden of Eden that God himself walks. He walks and talks with man! This walking and talking with Adam and Eve in the Garden may most easily be summarized as relationship, or even more succinctly, communion. The Catechism of the Catholic Church tells us that, "Man is made to live in communion with God in whom he finds happiness."[1] This is not the fleeting happiness of a delicious meal or a new car. No, this happiness found in communion with God is the soul-satisfying happiness that never fades.

---

[1] Catholic Church. (2000). *Catechism of the Catholic Church* (2nd Ed., p. 18). Washington, DC: United States Catholic Conference.

We are wired to seek peace and satisfaction, yes, even the joy that comes from this relationship, this communion with our Creator. Anything else is a poor and transitory substitute that will ultimately leave us lacking what we most desire. If we are to be truly happy, then we will live in communion with God. This was God's intent from the moment he created mankind. Not to abandon us as some would have us believe. Not to tease and test us, but to be in communion with his prize creation. Our Heavenly Father created us to be happy and complete in him! Our truest and deepest happiness is found only in living as God created us to live. St. Zélie Guérin Martin, the mother of St. Therese of Lisieux said, "never can that heart be satisfied which seeks anything but God."[2]

In fact, all of life is intended to be a journey back to this place of intimate fellowship, this communion with God himself! It is in this place of communion, in this relationship with the loving and merciful Creator of all, it is here that we find purpose and significance, that we find satisfaction. This is the communion that is described by St. Paul in his letter to the Ephesians as being represented by the intimacy of marriage, a complete and total giving of oneself to another so that the relationship makes two as one. In his Son, God gave totally of himself so that all who will receive his gift of saving grace can be the Bride of Christ, the church of the redeemed. St. Paul explains that he is not speaking only of earthly marriage, but even more profoundly, he speaks of a great mystery. The mystery of Christ and the Church, his body.

[2] Thérèse of Lisieux, S., & Taylor, T. N. (1912). *The Story of a Soul* (p. 6). London: Burns and Oates.

The unity experienced by Adam and Eve was perfect unity with each other, and perfect unity with God. This is why there was no shame, though they were naked. That perfect unity precluded any shame or animosity. Peace was the result of this unity. Man and woman, together in complete peace! This is what marriage is to be when "a man leaves his father and his mother and clings to his wife, and they become one flesh" (Gen. 2:24). Just imagine a marriage of peace, of perfect unity, truly one! This is God's intent for our relationships with each other and, most importantly, our relationship with Him. Of course, sin destroyed all this and the perfect peace and unity of man and God. Throughout all human history, God has been working to redeem mankind and to bring us back to this place of union with Him. He wants to bring us back because this is where we belong. This is where we began; the story of humanity begins in union with God. This was true in the Garden of Eden for Adam and Eve.

Chapter 2

The Garden Temple

The Garden is a unique place of God's presence.
(J. Daniel Hayes)

Ezekiel calls Eden, "the garden of God" (Ezek. 28:13). An incredibly special place on the holy mountain of God. Throughout Scripture, mountains are very special places. After the flood, the ark comes to rest on a mountain. A ram is offered as a substitute for the sacrifice of Abraham's son, Isaac, on Mt. Moriah. God meets Moses on the mountain to deliver the law. Solomon's Temple is built on Mt. Moriah. Jesus overcomes temptation on a mountain, he withdraws to a mountain to pray, gives the Beatitudes on a mountain, and is transfigured on a mountain. Jesus is arrested in a garden on a mountain and is crucified on Mt. Moriah.

Mountains are places where important things happen! In almost all ancient cultures mountains are associated with holy places. The thought that there is one primordial cosmic mountain that is the center of the earth, or *axis mundi*, is found in most ancient belief systems. Even to this day, many religions look to a "holy mountain" of some sort. For many, the *axis mundi* is the intersection of heaven and earth and even hell. In the Garden of Eden, we certainly see each of these elements. In considering the Garden on the holy mountain of God, we realize that this Garden is the temple of God. This is the place where God dwells with mankind. We know that the temple is the place where God establishes his dwelling among us. The psalmist calls out the "mount which God desired for his abode, yes, where the LORD will dwell forever. . ." (Ps. 68:16).

Scripture gives us indications that Eden is the original "temple" of God on this holy mountain. (And as we will explore later, Eden is a prefigurement of the Garden of Paradise, Heaven, itself!) Isn't it interesting that Genesis 2:2 speaks of gold and precious stones near Eden. This gives another clue about the Garden of Eden being God's Great Temple where He would dwell with mankind.

These precious materials were needed for the adornment of temples. The onyx was a "sacred stone" and often used for liturgical vessels and ornamentation of vestments. Even the rivers flowing out of Eden are indicative of the temple status of the Garden. Ezekiel 47 tells us, "water was issuing from below the threshold of the temple toward the east (for the temple faced east)" (Ezek. 47:1).

The entry into Eden was in the east. The eastern orientation of the entry was common for temples and was a feature of the temple of Solomon. For many centuries Christian churches were built so the altar was on the eastern end of the church. The priest and the people were *ad orientem,* facing east. Christians traditionally turned to the east to pray. (Not so much anymore, but that may be our loss.) Eden was to the east, the return of Christ will be from the east. Each of these details help us to understand that Eden was God's temple. The place of His dwelling.

God has always intended to dwell with mankind. He, from the moment of creation, has intended for you and me to be in an intimate relationship of life-giving communion with him. It is this communion of life that Jesus is speaking about when he tells us, "I am the vine, you are the branches. He who abides in me, and I in him, he it is that bears much fruit, for apart from me you can do nothing" (Jn 15:5). This is a relationship of unity, peace, and yes, blessing.

Throughout the Old Testament, we read of God amongst his people. In the Garden of Eden, he walked with Adam and Eve. In the wilderness, God dwelt with the Israelites in the Tabernacle. The Tabernacle was the tent that traveled with His chosen people on their journey to the Promised Land. This tent is described in rich detail in the Book of Exodus. The entire nation of Israel would camp in the wilderness with the Tabernacle in the center of the tribes.

The Tabernacle housed the Holy of Holies where God dwelt amongst His people. For nearly 500 years the dwelling of God with his people was in the Tabernacle. It is not until the reign of King Solomon that the Temple is finally built. Whether in a temporary tent, a splendid temple, or a lush Garden of abundance, God has always sought to dwell in the midst of his people. He tasks the Israelites with making a sanctuary, "that I may dwell in their midst"(Ex 25:8).

God is interested in more than just a literal physical dwelling place. Because he is God, he is not limited to one such place. St. Matthew quotes and clarifies the words of the prophet Isaiah when he records, "Behold, a virgin shall conceive and bear a son, and his name shall be called Emmanuel.' (which means, God with us)" (Mt 1:23). The very act of God sending his Son to be with us is the strongest statement of God's desire to dwell with mankind. St. John's Gospel tells us, "And the Word became flesh and dwelt among us, full of grace and truth; we have beheld his glory, glory as of the only-begotten Son from the Father" (Jn 1:14). God, in the incarnation of his Son, once again dwells with us!

Most importantly, God intends for us to be his temple, his dwelling place. We hear St. Paul declare, "Do you not know that you are God's temple and that God's Spirit dwells in you?" (1 Co 3:16). This is profound; we who were opposed to God have, by the redeeming work of Christ, become the very temple of God. St. John writes in his first letter, "Those who keep his commandments remain in him, and he in them, and the way we know that he remains in us is from the Spirit that he gave us" (1 Jn 3:24). God gave Adam and Eve only one restriction, one commandment as it were. They couldn't keep that one, and so God no longer dwelt with them (more about that later).

Through Christ Jesus, he now says he remains in all who keep his commands. In describing the Garden of Paradise, St. John writes, "Behold, the dwelling of God is with men. He will dwell with them, and they shall be his people, and God himself will be with them" (Rev. 21:3).

Chapter 3

The Garden of Abundance

And out of the ground the LORD God made to grow every tree that is pleasant to the sight and good for food. (Gen. 2:9)

As we read the biblical account of the Garden of Eden, we are in awe of the life that the Garden is filled with. God planted this garden. God made it to grow. Life is abundant in the Garden of Eden. In biblical Hebrew, *ʿēden*, means luxury, and delight and gives the impression of abundance. The Septuagint, a Greek translation of Hebrew Scriptures from the 2nd or 3rd century BC, literally translates the Garden of Eden in Genesis 3 as "the garden of luxuries." This fits with Genesis 2:9, "the LORD God made to grow every tree that is pleasant to the sight and good for food." Eden was surely a place of delight. Filled with fruit-bearing trees of all types, Eden was well-watered and beautiful to behold. Life in this paradise was filled with abundance.

In the middle of the garden were two trees so different from the others that they are identified by name, the "tree of life" and "the tree of the knowledge of good and evil." The luxury, delight, and abundance of the garden may best be summed up in the permission God gives to Adam and Eve, "You may freely eat of every tree of the garden; but of the tree of the knowledge of good and evil you shall not eat, for in the day that you eat of it you shall die" (Gen. 2:16–17). Think of that, Adam and Eve were clearly told that they could eat from every tree, including the tree of life! The only prohibition was the tree of knowledge of good and evil. All that Adam and Eve could want, or desire was in abundant supply in the Garden of Eden.

Because Eden is the temple of God, fullness, and abundance are what we expect to encounter. Remember that Eden is the place where God dwells with mankind. He walks with Adam and Eve in communion and friendship. The culmination of His creation, the one into whom He breathed the very breath of life, the one creature that "becomes a living soul" is placed in His Garden. God's plan for mankind was to have an abundant life.

This is what Jesus, the last Adam is speaking of when he says, "I came that they may have life, and have it abundantly" (Jn 10:10). Some hear these words and assume that our Christian life on earth should be filled with all kinds of good stuff. That attitude is so far from God's plan. The rich young ruler who came to Jesus found it very hard to leave his life of material comfort to follow Christ. How very important our stuff becomes to us. We even have a phrase for chasing all the things of the world; "keeping up with the Joneses." We live in a time of blatant consumerism. We are not far different from the writer of Ecclesiastes when he speaks of his vast possessions and pleasures as 'striving after the wind." There is no lasting happiness in the material goods of this world. More is not better. Abundance is not about possessions; abundance is about communion. Abundance is fellowship with God the Creator and Sustainer of all that is.

Fellowship with God is only possible in holiness and justice. Adam and Eve lived in this place of abundance. In their state of original holiness and justice, no good thing was lacking in their lives. In original justice, the state of perfect harmony, they knew no shame, they knew no disagreement, they knew no fear. They lived in the perfect love of God. "There is no fear in love, but perfect love casts out fear" (1 Jn 4:18). St. John also tells us that God is love. As Adam and Eve lived in the Garden of Eden, they existed in the perfect love that is God. It is not until Adam and Eve have sinned that they experience shame and fear. Up to that moment, all they knew was the perfect love of God! The Catechism of the Catholic Church says, "This grace of original holiness was to share in … divine life."[3] In all that they were, in all that they experienced, it was in this perfect love, in the divine life of God.

---

[3] Catholic Church, *Catechism of the Catholic Church*, 2nd Ed. (Washington, DC: United States Catholic Conference, 2000), 95.

This was the Garden of Eden, the Garden of Life. Adam and Eve did not experience the failings and frailties of the life that we now live. There was no war with pride. There was no manipulating and using others to get one's own way. Adam and Eve lived in perfect unity with God, with self, and with each other. They possessed the preternatural gifts of impassibility (freedom from pain), immortality (freedom from death), integrity (freedom from concupiscence, or disordered desires), and infused knowledge (freedom from ignorance in matters essential for happiness). Adam and Eve were not inclined to do evil. Their understanding and reason were not clouded by lust or pride. They had a perfect knowledge of moral law. They did not experience any conflict between the spirit and the body, and all the parts of the soul existed in a state of order and harmony. They were at peace with God, with self, and with others. The garden was a paradise that supported human life; their work was a source of pleasure and accomplishment. They were able to flourish to their fullest potential.

Scripture tells us of a river that waters the garden, and the river flows from the garden to the lands beyond. We will see this theme again when we look at the Garden of Paradise, but for now, we simply see the very waters of life flowing to water the garden. Without water, there is no life. Jesus told the woman at the well in the Gospel of St. John about living water. The river in Eden is like, "the river of the water of life, bright as crystal, flowing from the throne of God and of the Lamb through the middle of the street of the city" (Re 22:1–2). The river divides and flows to water the earth bringing life-giving water to otherwise parched lands.

Chapter 4

Man's Place in the Garden

The LORD God took the man and put him in the garden of Eden to till it and keep it. (Genesis 2:15)

It may seem like Adam and Eve were on a perennial vacation in a lush, delightful, luxurious paradise! I can almost see the two of them at this luxurious 5-star resort just relaxing, hanging out by the pool, sipping some adult beverages, and enjoying the tropical breezes. Except that's not at all the reality of the garden! God has a place and a purpose for them in the garden.

In creating Adam, God said, "Let us make man in our image, after our likeness" (Gen. 1:26). This is our first clue in understanding God's plan for mankind. It does us well to reflect for just a moment on the opening words of the Catechism of the Catholic Church, "God, infinitely perfect and blessed in himself, in a plan of sheer goodness freely created man to make him share in his own blessed life."[4] The clearest expression of what God intended for His premier creation was a sharing in God's own blessed life! The title of this section of the Catechism says succinctly, "THE LIFE OF MAN—TO KNOW AND LOVE GOD."[5] God wants us to know him intimately, he wants us to love him completely. He intends for us to be his children; his sons, and daughters! We read in Genesis 5:3 that Adam had a son named Seth. Seth was a son in "his own likeness, after his image" (Ge 5:3). Just as Seth was a son in the "image and likeness" of his father Adam, so Adam is a son in the "image and likeness" of his father. And so, you and I are made to be God's sons and daughters. This is God's plan at its very core.

Through Jesus Christ, the new Adam, "to all who received him, who believed in his name, he gave power to become children of God; who were born, not of blood nor of the will of the flesh nor of the will of man, but of God" (Jn 1:12–13).

---

[4] Catholic Church, *Catechism of the Catholic Church*, 2nd Ed. (Washington, DC: United States Catholic Conference, 2000), 7.
[5] Catholic Church, *Catechism of the Catholic Church*, 2nd Ed. (Washington, DC: United States Catholic Conference, 2000), 7.

That's powerful! Sons and daughters of God. With all the rights and responsibilities of family. God's plan for mankind is to be family. You and I, according to St. Paul's letter to the Romans, are "God's children, heirs of God and fellow heirs with Christ" (Ro 8:17). This is what God intended for all mankind to be, his children. Not outcasts, or those without a place at the family table, but adopted sons and daughters of God. Can you imagine being a fellow heir with Jesus Christ? To share in His glory? What a great calling God has given to us.

Next, let's look at what Adam was to do. "The LORD God took the man and put him in the garden of Eden to till it and keep it" (Ge 2:15). Adam was to tend to the garden. Remember that the Garden of Eden is God's temple. Who takes care of God's temple? His priests. The first thing that mankind was created to do was to take care of God's temple and to be his priests. I know you are thinking how did we get from tending the garden to being priests? The literal translation of "to till" is "work" or "serve" (abad) and "keep it" is "guard" (shamar). These are the same words used to describe what the Levitical priests did in the Tabernacle (Num 3:7-8; 8:26; 18:7), the temple that traveled with the children of Israel. The work described here is not solely pulling weeds or other tasks in the garden. No, much more is implied. This is the same word used when Moses hears God speaking as a burning bush. God told Moses that when the Children of Israel came out of Egypt Moses would "abad" or serve God on this very mountain! When Moses asks Pharoah to let God's people go, it is to go into the wilderness so that they may "abad" or serve God. We hear this same idea in the writings of St. Paul when he speaks of serving the Lord. Most poignantly, Jesus quotes the Decalogue and says, "It is written, 'You shall worship the Lord your God, and him only shall you serve'" (Lk 4:8). As God's adopted children we are called to do the work of tending to God's temple, whether that temple is the garden of Eden, the Tabernacle in the wilderness, Solomon's temple in Jerusalem, or the temple that is our very being.

All of this tells us that Adam was the priest in God's Garden temple. Not only is Adam a son of God, but he is also a priest of God.

Adam is also given the kingly job of dominion over all the living things of the earth. Just as the king reigns over his domain, Adam was to be the king of creation. We usually think of kings as despotic, overbearing, and demanding of their subjects. This is not the kind of king Adam is to be. Adam, and by extension all of mankind was to act as God's ambassador extending God's love and blessing to all the earth. And of course, the first place we must establish dominion is over our own misplaced and corrupted desires.

The last major role we must consider is Adam as the first prophet of God. A prophet speaks for God. Adam speaks the names of the animals in Genesis. While this doesn't seem like a big deal, in the ancient world only the creator of something, whether it was a piece of art, a piece of music, or even a child, had the right to name that creation. This was a really big deal! God assigned this task to Adam who would be the mouthpiece of God. Adam was God's prophet. This is what Jesus is speaking of in St. Luke's Gospel, "The good man out of the good treasure of his heart produces good, and the evil man out of his evil treasure produces evil; for out of the abundance of the heart his mouth speaks. (Luke 6:45). Our words matter. We speak for God, or we speak against Him.

Adam, the adopted son of God, was to be prophet, priest, and king. He is to take care of God's temple. He is to proclaim the love of his Father to all creation, bringing all creation into this intersection of heaven and earth. Sounds familiar doesn't! God calls Israel to be a nation of priests (Ex. 19:6). Jesus, as the new Adam, fulfills all three offices perfectly. St Peter tells us that as Christians, "you are a chosen race, a royal priesthood, a holy nation, God's own people" (1 Pe 2:9).

God's own people, you and I, are his prophets, his priests, and kings, ruling with Christ forever. Unfortunately, we know all too well what happened in the Garden. The intersection of heaven and earth was invaded by hell.

Chapter 5

Paradise Lost

It was not the apple on the tree but the pair on the ground that caused the trouble in the garden of Eden.
(Elizabeth Barrett Browning)

Before paradise can be lost, it must first be yours. And paradise truly was Adam and Eve's. Everything they could need was provided. Yes, Eden was paradesio, the intersection of heaven and earth, the place where God and man walked together in blessed communion. Until it wasn't. Genesis tells us of the serpent, the tempter, who speaks to Eve, sowing seeds of doubt. Seeds of disbelief.

The serpent asks with a sense of incredulity, "Did God say, 'You shall not eat of any tree of the garden? (Ge 3:1). As Satan always does, he undermines our relationship, our communion with God. Satan knew that was not God's command. He also always has his own alternative "truth." Of course, alternative truth is just another way of denying the truth, of speaking lies. And Satan is the father of lies.

It is important to note that Satan uses the term "*Elohim*" to refer to God. This was a less personal word for God than is used in Genesis 3:1, "the LORD God." Another way to interpret "LORD God" is Jehovah, or Yahweh. The LORD God is a very personal name for God. This is clear in Psalm 19. The first 6 verses refer to Elohim and his relationship with the material world. In the seventh verse, the psalmist refers to Yahweh and his relationship with those who know him in a covenantal relationship. Satan's first line of attack is to undermine the fact that Adam and Eve have a familial relationship with God, and that they are his own people. He will always make you doubt that God loves you as his precious child.

Satan always sows seed of doubt. Seeds of disbelief. He plants thoughts that undermine God's credibility. He is expert at playing us for his own evil purposes. Satan NEVER wants what is best for you. Let me say that again, Satan NEVER wants what's best for you. He will always seek to convince you that God doesn't either. Tragically for Adam and Eve, tragically for us, when we buy into Satan's lies we disobey God.

And that disobedience, that sin, breaks our unity with God. Death is the payment for disobedience. St. Paul tells us, "the wages of sin is death" (Rom. 6:23).

Satan makes some incredible promises to Eve. The first promise is that she will not die. As is almost always the case, what Satan says is the exact opposite of what God has declared. Satan casts doubt on God's love, his trustworthiness, and on His word. Up to this moment, Adam and Eve had no reason to fear death. They were created with preternatural gifts of divine grace that included bodily immortality! The Tree of Life was readily available to them in the Garden and there was no prohibition from eating from it. According to St. Paul, death came into the world, not by the hand of God, but rather, by the sin of Adam. In this moment the Garden that was full of abundance and life became a place of death. Eve has become the mother of death.

The second promise Satan makes to Eve is about sight, "your eyes will be opened." Satan is essentially telling Eve that she can't yet see all that is. She needs her eyes to be opened! It is worth noting that the ultimate end of mankind, the ultimate happiness of mankind is found in what the Catechism calls the "Beatific vision," the immediate knowledge of God that the angels and the souls of the just enjoy in heaven. This "vision" is different from the knowledge of God that the human mind may attain in the present life, for in beholding God face to face man finds perfect happiness, the vision is termed "beatific." One of the great promises of Scripture is that we shall see Him face to face! Before the Fall, Adam and Eve walked with God, talked with God, and saw God.

Rather than having her eyes opened, Eve was blinded by sin. This is the human condition, blinded, at best seeing shapes and shadows. Unable to truly see. Unable to actually perceive. Satan promised sight, he gave blindness. This blindness haunts humanity throughout Scripture. Think of the Children of Israel standing on the banks of the Jordan river, gazing into the promised land, the land that flows with milk and honey.

The promised land, the land of life and abundance. The land of freedom from slavery. And yet their eyes were blinded. Ten of the twelve spies sent into the land reported that in comparison to the inhabitants of that land, they seemed like grasshoppers in their own eyes. We read of the problem of sight in the story of the anointing of David as king of Israel. Samuel, the great prophet of God, looks at the sons of Jesse. He measures them by appearance and is stunned when God rejects everyone who looks kingly and anoints the young man, David. God goes so far as to declare, "the LORD sees not as man sees" (1 Sa 16:7). Eve lost her sight that day in the Garden and sinful man has been stumbling along in blindness ever since.

Even today we hear of people going on vison quests and retreats, trying to see. To find themselves. Some sit for days in darkness, total sensory deprivation. Others use shamanistic rituals and drugs. All seeking for what God has promised but looking in all the wrong places.

The final promise Satan makes to Eve is, "you will be like God, knowing good and evil" (Ge 3:5). Remember that Adam is created in the image and likeness of God. When God formed Adam, it was the breath of life, God's breath that was breathed into Adam. This is markedly different than the animals. It is only Adam who became a living soul. This speaks to the closeness of God to his prime creation, mankind. Pope Benedict XVI says, "To be the image of God implies relationality."6 God has called Adam by name, Adam was God's. (See Isa. 43:1) Adam was loved by God. We must know that God created mankind out of and by his love. We hear the echo of this in the command to Adam and Eve to be "fruitful and multiply." Adam and Eve were to be present for each other in such a way that their love would be creative! The physical union of man and woman was to be primarily the most intimate giving of self, the ultimate act of love. From this giving of self would spring new life, a new relationship.

God created Adam and saw that it was very good. From Adam's rib, God created Eve and Adam responded with joy! Adam and Eve were "like" God in ways that Satan could not offer. They could be fully present for each other, and isn't this really what love is? To be fully present, fully known without shame or fear!

St. Pope John Paul II writes, "Love is therefore the fundamental and innate vocation of every human being."7 We are most like God when we give self totally to another. This is what St. Paul is speaking of in Ephesians 5 when he tells husbands to love their wives in the same way that Christ loved the Church, "and gave himself up for her." It is the living example of God's love when he sent his one and only Son to love mankind with such completeness that it cost the Son's life! St. Paul assures us that "Knowledge" puffs up, but love builds up" (1 Co 8:1). Adam and Eve were about to live that realization. Puffed up with the knowledge of good and evil, Adam and Eve's lives would now be filled with the consequences of evil. Good would be experienced only in fleeting moments.

Up to this moment, all Adam and Eve experienced was good. All that they knew was good. In reality, all that Satan could offer was the knowledge of evil. This lie would rob Adam and Eve of the pure vision of nothing but good. Good in themselves, in the created things around them, and, most importantly, in God Himself. Now a new perspective would enter the equation. A perspective that was not as things really were, but rather as they would be without God and his sustaining love.

---

[6] Pope Benedict XVI, *"In the Beginning ...": A Catholic Understanding of the Story of Creation and the Fall*, trans. Boniface Ramsey, Ressourcement: Retrieval & Renewal in Catholic Thought (Grand Rapids, MI: William B. Eerdmans Publishing Company, 1995), 47.

Their submission to Satan and self would bring enmity with God and with others. Now hatred would run rampant. (Think Cain and Abel.) This is the alternate reality brought about by sin. They would know evil. That evil would cause shame and fear. It would bring turmoil, suffering and pain. Having let trust in God die in his heart, Adam forgot Him from whom he had received life. By seeking life apart from the Giver of Life, Adam found only death and separation from his Creator.

Evil introduced a fragility that would undercut the abundance of the Garden and substitute scarcity. A fragility that would cause the weeds to overwhelm the crops. A fragility of life that would end in death. It is this broken, disordered reality that sin would unleash upon the world and all mankind.

Remember the childhood game of hide and seek? While Adam and Eve were doing their best to hide from God, He was seeking for them. Listen to the words of Scripture:

> And they heard the sound of the LORD God walking in the garden in the cool of the day, and the man and his wife hid themselves from the presence of the LORD God among the trees of the garden. But the LORD God called to the man, and said to him, "Where are you?" And he said, "I heard the sound of you in the garden, and I was afraid, because I was naked; and I hid myself. (Gen. 3:8–10)

Listen to all that has been lost! They hid themselves from the presence of God. Before the Fall, they enjoyed relationship, communion, the presence of the Lord. In hiding from God, they also hid from each other. Suddenly they realize they are naked or uncovered. So, they make a poor attempt at covering their nakedness. Where they had once been covered by the perfect love of God, they now are "freed" by knowledge that is not founded in love, but in selfishness.

---

[7] John Paul II, *Familiaris Consortio* (Vatican City: Libreria Editrice Vaticana, 1981).

So much of our lives are filled with this same selfishness. From our earliest days our choices and our actions are centered in the great lie of Me. It is all about me. I am the center of my universe. All exists for me. No, we never say it quite like that, but it is proven by our priorities and actions.

Adam and Eve lost those preternatural gifts of grace. No longer immortal, no longer free from passions that are disordered. Mankind was no longer free from suffering. All because his life that had consisted of his union with God as the source, the Creator of his life was now broken. Now Adam would find that in himself, life was very hard. His freedom was gone. How often do we associate freedom with the ability to do whatever we want! Yet freedom is in being all that God created us to be, free from sin. In communion with Him. Now Adam would be driven by the need to eke out an existence until the inevitable day of death knocked on his door.

Many years ago, I drove by my grandmother's old house. She didn't live there anymore and had now completed her journey of life on this earth. So much had changed. Grandmother's garden was no longer evident. People I didn't know now called that old house home. All that remained for me were memories. Memories of games of tag played with cousins, of hide and seek played in the gloaming. I could almost hear the sounds of laughter, the conversations around the table as grandma dished out her fabulous chicken and dumplings followed by homemade banana pudding for dessert. No matter how much I would have liked to go back to those "good old days," everything had changed.

This is a bit of what it must have been for Adam and Eve as God banished them from the Garden. With the realization that everything had changed, they had no way back to where they had been. Not back to where they had been with each other, with creation, and, most of all with God. The intimacy, the friendship, the freedom, the peace was all just memories. No longer centered in God and his love.

No longer able to freely eat from the abundance that God provided, Adam and Eve were banished from the Garden. Angels and a flaming sword now guarded the entrance to the place where they had walked and talked with God. They could not go back. How tragic it would be if the story had ended there. But God had a plan.

Section 2

God, The Constant Gardener

God never gives up on us. If He wanted to quit, He would have given up way back in the garden of Eden. (Anonymous)

Chapter 6

God's Love Moves Him to Constantly Search for Us

He was seeking for me, seeking for me, Tho' I knew Him not. Still He loved me, And was seeking for me. (Lanny Wolfe)

Adam and Eve had through their distrust, their pride, their disobedience rejected their familial relationship as the children of God. Where there had been life, laughter, and love there was now a vast gulf. A divide that mankind could never bridge.

Yet God, from the very moment of Adam and Eve's sin, promised to bridge that gap, to once again give to all who would receive it, the power to be sons and daughters of God. To once again be His people. To again know the joy, peace, and freedom found only in the perfect love of God. You see God is the constant gardener, the One who seeks the harvest of souls, that we might again share in His blessed life. The Catechism makes this clear, "Although man can forget God or reject him, He never ceases to call every man to seek him, so as to find life and happiness."[8]

God is calling you and me. In the words of an old gospel song, He is calling for us to come home. He calls us to come home to him. To come back to where He intended us to be from the moment that He breathed life into mankind. Everything that has come since the Fall is about God bridging the great divide caused by sinful disobedience, by selfish pride. Everything is to draw us to Him, back to the Garden of Paradise. He wants to offer us a share in His blessed life, to be His adopted sons and daughters. This is what Jesus said was His mission, the reason he came, "For the Son of man came to seek and to save the lost" (Lk 19:10).

Jesus, the Promised One of Genesis 3:15, came to do the will of His Father. Remember that "it is not the will of your heavenly Father that one of these little ones be lost" (Mt 18:14). The LORD God wants you and I to come home. Not just as visitors who spare a few minutes a week for Him, but as those who live in constant communion with Him.

---

[8] Catholic Church, Catechism of the Catholic Church, 2nd Ed. (Washington, DC: United States Catholic Conference, 2000), 14.

To this end, God has revealed Himself, and His love for us throughout salvation history. God is the Father who is continually and systematically bringing man toward his redemption. He has become the Way back to the Garden.

God, working through His chosen people Israel, began the long process of bringing us home. As we read the Old Testament, we are reading the story of God the Father continually, patiently, working to bring mankind to redemption. He does this because He is love. Not some passing feeling, not some self-serving emotion, God is love.

So often we speak of this love of God from our perspective of what love is. Remember that at the moment of Adam and Eve's disobedience, the human understanding of love changed. Suddenly they were afraid. They were ashamed. Their children knew hatred and envy. Love became something that is self-serving, self-promoting, and self-fulfilling. How different than God, who is love. St. Paul tells us that "Why, one will hardly die for a righteous man—though perhaps for a good man one will dare even to die. But God shows his love for us in that while we were yet sinners Christ died for us" (Rom 5:7–8). While we were yet sinners . . . what a thought! While we were in sin and fearful shame, living the sin curse of Adam and Eve, God has shown his love for us. How did He show his love for us? By sending His one and only Son to die for us!

Jesus himself said that "Greater love has no man than this, that a man lay down his life for his friends. You are my friends if you do what I command you" (Jn 15:13–14). Jesus was telling his disciples that in just a few hours he would, by his actions, define the love that God is. It is this agape, best described in 1 Corinthians 13, that is God acting through the ages to bring us home to him. Because of this love, this self-giving, self-sacrificing love, Jesus says that those who obey his commandments are now his friends. This love is the greatest commandment.

In the Old Testament the phrase loving-kindness, from the Hebrew *chesed,* speaks of God's everlasting, changeless love. Nothing that Adam and Eve had done, nothing that you or I can ever do will change the love of God towards us. For you see, this steadfast love, this loving-kindness is a covenantal love. The sacramental love of holy matrimony is representative of this love. The bride and the bridegroom enter into an unbreakable covenant. Jeremiah the prophet records God speaking, "I have loved you with an everlasting love; therefore I have continued my faithfulness to you" (Jer. 31:3). These words were spoken to the children of Israel who have been taken captive by a foreign power because of their sinfulness. Yet through it all, God says he will come for them, restore them and they will be his people. Why? Because God has always been searching for, seeking those who will respond to His love and love him entirely.

Because of this immeasurable love for us, God has been seeking for us, searching for us and calling us, much as He did Adam and Eve on that fateful day in the Garden of Eden. Jesus explains God's seeking for us most clearly in the 15th chapter of St. Luke's Gospel. Jesus shares 3 parables, each a story of seeking that which is lost.

First, He tells the story of the shepherd who has a missing sheep. Ninety-nine sheep are accounted for, one is missing. The shepherd goes after the one that is lost. He searches until he finds it. This is the Good Shepherd, the Shepherd of David's great psalm. The Lord, who is my Shepherd comes searching for me, searching for you, the one lost sheep. This is the loving-kindness, the mercy that is God's love. At the finding of the lost one, heaven is filled with rejoicing.

In the parable of the lost coin, Jesus tells us that the woman who has lost one of her ten coins searches diligently. She lights a lamp; she sweeps the house until she finds the one lost coin. And just like the parable of the lost sheep, Jesus tells his listeners that, there is joy before the angels of God over one sinner who repents" (Lk 15:10). This is the heart of the Lord God towards his prize creation, you and me. But the story that really hits home is the story of the lost son.

We often call this the parable of the prodigal son, but if we look closely, we will also see the parable of the loving father. The younger son, like so many young men, desires to be his own man. By asking for his share of the family inheritance, this son is basically saying that he wishes dad would just die and be done with it. He is in effect saying, "you're dead to me." He leaves his father's house. He cuts himself off from his family, and their support.

He, like Adam and Eve, listens and responds to the siren's song of temptation. The younger son is no longer under the care and protection of his father, but he feels free! He no longer has a home, but as long as his money holds out, he is a very popular guy! He doesn't know it, but the happiness he feels, it's just the happiness of the moment, the happiness that money does buy! That kind of happiness is a bit like the happiness of a really good Thanksgiving dinner! Sumptuous food, delicious desserts, and way too much of all of it! We eat and eat and eat some more!

And then as always happens, sin demands its due. We develop a belly ache from overindulgence. Happiness is now but a memory. The illusory freedom becomes abject misery. The stomach once full of the unsatisfying fruit of selfishness is now growling with pangs of starvation. The once proud young man is reduced to not only feeding the swine but even longing to eat the leftover pig slop. Talk about "sweat of your brow" time! This young man is a picture of all who reject their rightly ordered place in the family of God. Things may go well for a bit, but ultimately sin always costs everything. And most costly of all, is your place at the family table, your place in God's house.

"That son . . . in a certain sense is the man of every period, beginning with the one who was the first to lose the inheritance of grace and original justice. The parable indirectly touches upon every breach of the covenant of love, every loss of grace, every sin."[9] Just like Adam and Eve, it would be terrible if that were the end of the story.

The younger son, living in exile, hungry, destitute, comes to himself and decides to go back to the only home he has ever had. Not the racy life in that far away country where "home" was just an illusion. No, he would return to the house of his father. Not as a son. Not as one with privileges and blessing, but as a hired hand, a servant.

This son has left the father's house of abundance, a house where there is "bread enough and to spare." This reminds us of the abundance of the Garden of Eden. God the Father had offered Adam and Eve, and through them, all mankind His abundant supply. All that was lost when sin entered in, but the Father seeks those who will receive life and "that more abundantly." And so, the son returns, to be a slave, a servant, the least in his father's house where there is abundance.

What happens next in the parable reveals the loving, forgiving heart of God. Even through the pain of rejection, and the darkness of separation, it is clear that the father has never given up looking for his son. The very day that the son returns Scripture tells us that the father saw his son, even though his son was still some distance away.

The picture I see in my mind is of a large estate at the top of a gently sloping tree-lined lane. I imagine the father walking down the lane every day, straining to see as far down the old country road as he could. Wondering "is this the day that my son might return? Is this the day that the one who is dead to me finds life, the hour in which he is lost no more?" The father's friends and his family, in their lack of understanding, no doubt shook their heads at the old man.

[9] John Paul II, *Dives in Misericordia* (Vatican City: Libreria Editrice Vaticana, 1980).

"Why doesn't he just give it up? The younger son is not worth this grief, this prolonged agony." But the father knew his son, even at a distance. Our Father has always known us in spite of the separation of sin.

The father had "compassion." This compassion is the heart of God. Exodus tells us that the Lord God is "compassionate and merciful, slow to anger, and abounding in faithfulness and truth, who keeps faithfulness for thousands, who forgives wrongdoing, violation *of His Law,* and sin. . ." (Ex 34:6–7). This is the compassion that causes Jesus to open blind eyes (See Matthew 20:29ff). It is this compassion that moves Jesus when he sees the people "like sheep without a shepherd" (Mark 6:34). And yes, it is this compassion that moves Jesus to feed the multitudes.

The compassion the father has for his son moves the father to run toward his son. The compassion that God has for his lost children caused him to run toward us through Jesus.

Then the father embraces and kisses his son. In that culture, the embrace, and the kiss were signs of love, acceptance, and forgiveness. The father's love for his sin had never faltered, never waned. Through the dark nights of lovingly longing for his son to come home, the father had never loved his son any less. No matter how far from home we have roamed, no matter the wrongdoing, the violation of His law, no matter the sin, God the compassionate, merciful, Father, full of loving-kindness towards us offers the embrace and kiss of forgiveness to all who return to His home.

When Adam and Eve succumbed to the temptation of the Deceiver, they realized they were naked. No longer clothed in God's grace and mercy, they tried to make coverings for themselves out of leaves from a fig tree. Isn't it a bit coincidental that they tried to use parts of a tree to cover themselves? Their innocence was lost by eating the fruit of a tree and it is on a tree where God's only begotten Son who will become the covering for all who respond to God's call is sacrificed.

For now, God covers them with the skins of an animal.

Some early church fathers equate the covering in the skins of an animal with the loss of sonship, no longer adorned in the robes of God's grace and righteousness. The father in Luke 15 calls for the best robe to clothe his son, once lost, but now found. Not the robe of a servant, but the "best robe." No longer clothed in the rags of a swine herder but now adorned in the robes of the father!

The book of Zechariah records a vision that sheds light on the significance of this moment. "Now Joshua was standing before the angel, clothed with filthy garments. And the angel said to those who were standing before him, "Remove the filthy garments from him." And to him, he said, "Behold, I have taken your iniquity away from you, and I will clothe you with rich apparel" (Zec. 3:3–4). Joshua, the son of Jozadak was the high priest who led the priests in rebuilding the temple and restoring the sacrifices and festivals. In other words, he was instrumental in bringing God's chosen people, back from their lives apart from God.

Isaiah speaks of the ministry of Christ in Isaiah 61. We are told of an "everlasting covenant" that the Lord God shall make with His chosen people. He will clothe them "with the garments of salvation" and cover them "with the robe of righteousness. This is how God will clothe those who return to him. The son, dressed in rags, is restored to "rich apparel."

The ring was a sign of authority for the family. When the father placed the ring on his once-dead son, he gave him restored authority. Finally, the father says to put shoes on his feet. To be without shoes was a sign of destitution. Only the poorest, and most destitute, were without shoes. The son is rescued from the destitution of sin, from the separation from his father, and restored to the house of abundance.

And just like the parables of the lost coin and the lost sheep, it is time for rejoicing. The father called for the fatted calf to be offered up as a feast, it was time to make merry.

Not in "riotous" living, but in a celebration of life found! This is how our Heavenly Father seeks us. This is how He receives us. This is how He restores us. To those "who received him, who believed in his name, he gave power to become children of God" (Jn 1:12).

It has been like this since the Fall in the Garden. God has been looking for all who would believe. Adam and Eve and all who sin, distrust God. Only those who respond in faith believing receive that "power" to become God's children.

Chapter 7

God Reveals Himself and His Love through Covenants

Again and again you called us into covenant with you.
(Eucharistic Prayer IV)

God, the constant Gardner, ever searching for His lost sheep, is not motivated by desperation, but rather by the intensity and urgency of love. Just as a man and a woman bind themselves together to become one flesh, God repeatedly binds Himself to his people by covenants. These covenants, sealed with ritual words, ritual actions, and sacrifice (see Ps. 50:5), promise fidelity and provision. Not mere contracts, but the indissoluble, "solemn agreement between human beings or between God and a human being involving mutual commitments or guarantees."[10] These covenants are the major moments that move forward the work of God to bring about salvation and the restoration of the relationship, the communion He intended to have with mankind.

5 major covenants are our guide through God's revealing Himself, and His plan to retore mankind to their right relationship with Himself. These covenants are the step-by-step process of God restoring sight to mankind. These covenants are the framework of the Old Testament. By the way, it is worth noting that we regularly refer to the Sacred Scriptures as having an Old Testament and a New Testament. Testament is another word for covenant. The first portion of Scripture is the Old Covenant that is fulfilled in Christ, followed by the New Covenant, Christ Himself!

As God seeks to reveal Himself, to reveal His love for mankind, He binds Himself to mankind in these five covenants. Each covenant comes with commitments and curses. We will see this most clearly in God's covenant with Abraham. The covenants that God makes with mankind are all part of His plan to restore you and me to His family. To put the "best robes" once again upon our shoulders! To welcome us home with great rejoicing!

---

[10] Catholic Church, *Catechism of the Catholic Church*, 2nd Ed. (Washington, DC: United States Catholic Conference, 2000), 873.

God's Covenant with Adam

His covenant with Adam is seen in the marriage of Adam and Eve and further confirmed in the *protoevangelium* (the first Gospel) when God declares that he will "put enmity between you and the woman, and between your seed and her seed; he shall bruise your head, and you shall bruise his heel" (Ge 3:15). Though God curses the ground, He does not curse Adam and Eve.

In His divine, loving mercy, God promises immediately after the Fall to restore, not abandon, His prize creation. He will once again, by the Holy Spirit, breathe the breath of life into each one who receives the gift of God's grace unto salvation. It is God who made "garments of skins" for Adam and Eve as a covering for their nakedness and shame. This implies the first sacrificial offering of life, the shedding of blood because of sin. As we will see, each of the covenants that reveal God's constant work to bring us back home require the sacrifice of the life of a blameless victim for the atonement of sin. As we will soon see, this sacrificial victim was most properly a lamb.

God's Covenant with Noah

It didn't take long for sin to become so rampant on the earth that the earth was corrupt in God's sight (Gen. 6). Yet God found one man who was righteous. Scripture tells us that Noah walked with God. This reminds us of Adam and Eve who also walked with God. Because of Noah's righteousness, God spares Noah and his family from the impending destruction of the world by flood.

After the Ark finally comes to rest on dry land, God makes a covenant with Noah. In this covenant, there is a renewal of creation. As the earth was in Genesis 1, so the earth is after the flood. It is as if the earth is a blank canvas for God to start His dealings with mankind all over. And Noah, a righteous man is the center of this work. Oh, and by the way, Noah is also a type of Christ.

The ark is filled with animals, a new Eden if you will. The ark lands on a new mountain, Ararat, and sacrifice is made on this mountain. Just like the waters of baptism, from which we arise as a new creation in Christ, so the world was washed and cleansed from the sinfulness that had overwhelmed the earth by the flood.

Like Adam, Noah is told to "be fruitful and multiply, bring forth abundantly on the earth and multiply in it" (Ge 9:7). It is noteworthy that God repeats to Noah what mankind can eat. In the Garden of Eden, Adam and Eve were given permission to eat from every plant and tree (except the tree of knowledge of good and evil). Noah is given all the animals.

Adam could have eaten from the tree of life, but Noah is commanded to not consume blood because the blood is life. Sacrifice will require blood, and as we will see, only those who drink the blood that is shed on the tree of Calvary will have life (see John 6). Unfortunately, it doesn't take long before sin is once again rampant as mankind chooses its own way instead of God's way. And just like Eden, sin once again breaks mankind's communion with God.

An interesting event takes place at this point in Scripture, mankind decides to build a city with a tower that reaches into the heavens, a poor imitation of a holy mountain. Eden is lost and gone and again, mankind no longer walks with and talks with God but rather wants to make a name for themselves. Names are really important. Remember that Adam is given dominion and names all the animals. When we get to the Garden of Resurrection, we will be reminded of how important names are. For now, it is enough to be reminded that our name identifies us with our family. Our name tells whom we belong with and to whom we belong.

To make a name for oneself as described in Genesis 11 was to make a name apart from God. Apart from God is death. The people are seeking to secure their future by their own means. God once again must intervene. And so, He does. Languages are confused, identities are separated, and all the people are scattered. Once again relationships, communion is broken.

From this scattered humanity comes the story of a family who left everything they knew and traveled to a place that was unknown to them. Terah and his family, including Abram, Sarai, and Lot were going to Canaan. Canaan is what will become known as the Promised Land. It is a land of God's blessings. It flows with "milk and honey." Sadly, on their journey, the family "settled" in a place called Haran. Haran means road or path. Scholars believe that this ancient community was located at a junction of trade routes. Haran was at the crossroads.

Throughout life, we are faced with many crossroads. Junctions that require a choice, a change in direction. These crossroads moments are where hard choices are made. The decisions made have a cascading effect on our lives. Adam and Eve faced a crossroads moment when confronted by the serpent. Noah faced a crossroads moment when God commanded him to make an ark and fill it with the animals and his own family. Jesus faced a crossroads moment on the night He was betrayed. As we will focus on a bit later, crossroads decisions draw us into the Garden of Gethsemane. Terah settled at the crossroads. His journey to Canaan came to an end as he settled. How often our continuing conversion is stymied because we settle at a crossroads.

God's Covenant with Abraham

After Terah died in Haran, at the crossroads, God spoke to Abram. God told Abram, who will later become known as Abraham, to go:

> to the land that I will show you. And I will make of you a great nation, and I will bless you, and make your name great, so that you will be a blessing. I will bless those who bless you, and him who curses you I will curse; and by you all the families of the earth shall bless themselves. So, Abram went, as the LORD had told him. . . (Ge 12:1–4)

God promises Abram 3 things, a great name, a great nation, and a blessing for all the world.

As we read the story of Abram, God makes these promises into a covenant in the 15th chapter of Genesis. This covenant with Abram tells us of the people God will use to reveal His love to all mankind. These people, the descendants of Abraham, will be God's chosen people.

It will be through Abraham's son Isaac, a son born by the miraculous intervention of God, that we gain insight into how God will restore fellowship with mankind (See Genesis 17,18). Issac is the son of promise. A promise made by God. And it is through Abraham's obedience to God when called to sacrifice the very son of promise, that it is revealed that God will provide himself the lamb for a burnt offering (Ge 22:8).

God called to Abraham and told him to offer Isaac as a burnt offering on a mountain in Moriah. On Mt. Moriah Abraham is ready to offer his only-begotten son, the son whom he loves as an offering in obedience to God. The parallels with Jesus Christ, God's only-begotten, beloved Son are impossible to miss.

While there are many seemingly insignificant little details like Isaac carrying the wood for the sacrifice just as Jesus carried the wood of the cross of sacrifice, no detail is more significant than the submission of both Isaac and Jesus to the will of their fathers, even obedience unto death. What a stark contrast to the failure to submit wholly to the will of God, their Father, on the part of Adam and Eve.

Yet through all that, God, the constant Gardner, continued to reveal His love for His children through the very covenants that He instituted. After Abraham was obedient to God's call to sacrifice Isaac, Scripture tells us that God says he would indeed bless Abraham "because you have obeyed my voice" (Ge 22:18).

Here then is a key point to consider. Adam heard God's voice when he was given every tree in the garden to eat from except the one. Adam did not obey, but in disbelief discounted and ignored the voice of God and suffered the penalty of scarcity and death. Abraham hears God's voice and obeys, and God blesses Abraham. As God seeks after us, He seeks those who will hear His voice and obey.

Of course, all along this journey back to God, man has taken many, many detours. Often, we have disobeyed and outright rejected God. Yet in His constant love for us, God keeps calling. God keeps searching. God remains faithful. Like the shepherd with the one lost sheep or the father whose son is lost, He keeps searching for you and me.

God's Covenant with Moses

The love of God for his people turns his ear to the cry of His children of Israel who had been slaves in Egypt for 400 years. God came to "deliver them out of the hand of the Egyptians, and to bring them up out of that land to a good and broad land, a land flowing with milk and honey" (Ex 3:8). He came seeking to bring his people back to the land He had promised Abraham, Isaac, and Jacob (See Genesis 15, 46).

The words here are reminiscent of Eden. "Flowing with milk and honey" recalls the abundance in the Garden. It is this abundance, found in communion with Him, that God is calling His children back to.

While in Egypt, the Israelites had become comfortable with the gods of Egypt. They needed to be reminded that they were the chosen people of God. That it is through them that He will bless all nations with salvation and restoration to His family.

When we consider how God seeks after us, we can hear His love as He tells Moses what He is about to do for the sons of Israel:

"I will bring you out, I will deliver you, I will redeem you, I will take you for my people, I will be your God, I will bring you into the land, I will give it to you"(Ex 6:6–8).
While these words in Exodus 6 speak directly to the children of Israel in slavery and bondage in the land of Egypt, the same words could be spoken about God's workings through Christ Jesus for each one of us.

Throughout Scripture, Egypt is a type or representation of the world ruled by other gods. Slavery and bondage to sin and death are always a part of life in this picture of Egypt. God makes seven great "I will" statements. Each of these is so that we "shall know that I am the LORD your God" (Ex 6:7). God wants us to return to His original intent for us all, to know the Lord our God, to be His people.

God says He will bring us out from under the burdens of a sin-sick world. God says that He will deliver us from the bondage of sin. He says that He will redeem us with His outstretched arm! He will take us, a people who have no right, no claim, to be His own children. God Himself, the creator and master of all that exists will be our God. And He will give us the land of promise as our inheritance!

God wants to bring us into the land of promise, the Garden in His Presence. Ultimately, as we shall see, that Garden is the Garden of Paradise or Heaven. God declares "Behold, the dwelling of God is with men. He will dwell with them, and they shall be his people, and God himself will be with them" (Rev 21:3).

As the children of Israel leave Egypt and come to the base of Mt. Sinai, God speaks through Moses and makes a covenant with the children of Israel (See Genesis 19, 24). God lays out His way to the children of Israel in the Decalogue or Ten Commandments. He gives a bit more instruction and then says that if the people will do these things,

He will be their God and they will be His people, a prized possession among all people, a royal priesthood to all the nations, and a holy nation. (Remember Adam's jobs in the Garden of Eden?)

As the children of Israel leave Egypt and come to the base of Mt. Sinai, God speaks through Moses and makes a covenant with the children of Israel (See Genesis 19, 24). God lays out His way to the children of Israel in the Decalogue or Ten Commandments. He gives a bit more instruction and then says that if the people will do these things, He will be their God and they will be His people, a prized possession among all people, a royal priesthood to all the nations, and a holy nation. (Remember Adam's jobs in the Garden of Eden?)

As the blood of animals sacrificed is poured upon the altar and upon the people, the covenant is sealed. Yet within days, the children of Israel have forgotten the covenant, they have made a golden calf and returned to the ways of Egypt. (Man's behavior really haven't changed much.) Still, God does not give up, the constant Gardener continues to work His plan for the redemption of mankind.

God's Covenant with David

St. Matthew's Gospel opens with the words, "The book of the genealogy of Jesus Christ, the son of David, the son of Abraham" (Matt 1:1). This genealogy begins a tracing of the lineage of Christ from Abraham through David. While the genealogy continues through the lineage up to the birth of Christ, we will stop with King David.

David was the second king of Israel. Saul had failed miserably. And while David had his share of failures, he turned to God in repentance. David often wrote laments, psalms that describe the troubles of life. In these lament psalms, David expresses regret for his sins and seeks the healing forgiveness of God.

Listen to David cry out to God in Psalm 41, "O LORD, be gracious to me; heal me, for I have sinned against you!" (Ps 41:4). David regularly seeks God's forgiveness recognizing that "The LORD is near to the brokenhearted, and saves the crushed in spirit" (Ps 34:18).

It is through David's descendants that the Promised One spoken of in Genesis 3 will come. His kingdom will be everlasting. This is the covenant that God makes with David.

In a sense, this covenant is a continuation of, and refinement of the covenant God had made with Abraham. God had promised that through a son of Abraham the promise would flow. Now, God refines that promise to David, a descendant, or son, of Abraham, that David's son will sit on his throne forever. That son will be God's Son, God's King, and He will deliver God's people from the curse of sin. He will once again restore the communion, the relationship of peace and friendship with God. God says to David, "I will make with you an everlasting covenant, my steadfast, merciful love for David" (Isa. 55:3). As we have seen throughout the history of mankind, God is constantly seeking to restore all that was lost in that fateful moment of rebellion in the Garden of Eden.

Chapter 8

Jesus Christ, the New Adam

Jesus Christ, the son of David, the son of Abraham. (Matt. 1:1)

St. Paul tells us in Romans 5:14 that Adam was a prefigurement of the one who would come. A new Adam would set all things in order as God had originally intended.

This One, the Christ, would not succumb to the disobedience of the first Adam. Rather, this last Adam would remain faithful to the will of the One who sent him. The first Adam brought death, "sin came into the world through man and death through sin" (Rom. 5:12). The last Adam was obedient even to death, and not just any death, but "even death on a cross" (Philippians 2:8).

Through the death of the last Adam, life is given to all who will receive Him. St. Paul goes on to tell us that Christ's "act of righteousness" brings life for all men! It is worth noting that in his letter to the Philippians, St. Paul tells us that Jesus took the form of a servant. Jesus is "Emmanuel" which translates as "God with us." God came to be with us as a servant. He would serve all by seeking and saving the lost and dying. He came to restore life by overcoming the law of sin and death. This is what Jesus the Christ accomplishes through His life, death, and resurrection.

The perfect and sin-free Jesus declared Himself to be The Bread of Life in John 6. He said that we must eat His flesh and drink His blood to have eternal life. This reference to eating, of course, is the antidote to overcoming what Adam did. Jesus, who died on the tree of life known as the cross, commands us to eat the fruit from that tree (his flesh and blood), so as to give us eternal life and to overcome the lies of the devil to Adam. The devil said that if you eat the forbidden fruit, "You shall not die." By eating the fruit of the cross, the flesh and blood of Christ, "You shall live forever," said Jesus. "If you eat of the forbidden fruit", the devil said, "your eyes will be opened."

Yet, Adam's eyes were blinded, and he could no longer see God face to face. Jesus tells the disciples that if you have seen Christ, you have seen the Father. The blinded eyes were opened. The devil also told Adam that if he ate the forbidden fruit, he would be like God. Jesus said that if we eat His flesh and drink his blood, He will abide in us, and we in Him. We will be God's children.

The parallels between Adam and Jesus don't end there, though. Just as Adam was ejected from Paradise so that he could eventually be saved from his disobedient sin, Jesus came down from Paradise to the dwelling place of Adam (this world) to save us all from Adam's original sin. Just as Adam's disobedience to God allowed sin and damnation to enter the world, the obedience of the new Adam, Jesus, to God, His loving Father, brought salvation to the world. Just as Adam threw away his sinless status through disobedience, Jesus kept his sinless status through obedience.

In John 14:30, Jesus said that the devil is the ruler of this world. Jesus is the ruler of the everlasting world, in Heaven. Just as the devil once conquered man in Paradise, the dwelling place of God, now, Jesus, a man who is not only like God, but who IS God, conquers the devil in his dwelling place, this world.

As Jesus suffered his Passion, the curse of Adam, namely sweat on his brow and thorns, was placed squarely on the head of Christ, the Bread of Life, first in the Garden of Gethsemane, when he sweat blood, and then in Jerusalem, when he had a crown of thorns placed on His head. Whereas Adam was naked and had to put clothes on because of his disobedience, Jesus, through His obedience to God, was clothed on the way to Calvary, and then stripped naked before crucifixion. Adam fell because of the wooden tree of knowledge of good and evil; Jesus fell under the weight of the wooden cross, the instrument of torture and death. God breathed the breath of life into mankind; Jesus suffocated on the cross through the actions of mankind.

Adam was created in a state of communion with God. Until the Fall, Adam was without sin. Until the Fall, Adam would not taste death. Because of the Fall, because of sin, because of disobedience of God's command, Adam was condemned to death. That death was at once instantaneous by means of separation from God as we read of in Revelation 20:6. No longer was mankind in perfect communion with his Creator. No longer did Adam walk and talk with God in peace and friendship. Now there was enmity, now there was separation, life was gone, death now reigned.

Let's be really clear about this! Sacred Scripture tells us that we are earning a paycheck for our lives. You are, I am. That paycheck is death. "For the wages of sin is death" (Rom. 6:23). In that same chapter of his letter to the Romans, St. Paul reminds us that we are either slaves to sin and death or slaves to righteousness in Christ Jesus. One ends in death, the other in God's free gift, eternal life! This is the Gospel of God. The Good News! This is the manifest purpose of God, the mystery of His will, and His "plan for the fulness of time, to unite all things in him (Christ), things in heaven and things on earth" (Eph. 1:10).

St. Paul goes on to tell the Ephesians that we have been brought near to God in Christ Jesus. We are no longer separated from Him, rather the very blood of Christ has brought all who will receive His saving grace into the very family of God. Just like Adam and Eve started out. Just as God had intended from the beginning. God never wanted separation; God never wanted death for any. Scripture tells us that God does not want anyone to perish. He wants us to come back to Him. He wants to restore all that sin has destroyed the peace, the harmony, the relationships, and the communion that mankind shared with God in the Garden.

This is why Jesus Christ, Emmanuel, "God with Us" comes to earth. The only way back to the Garden of God is through Jesus Christ. Jesus himself tells us,

"I am the way, and the truth, and the life; no one comes to the Father, but by me" (Jn 14:6). The only way back to where we started, the only way back to where God intended, the only way to where we experience the joy and abundance that we were made for is through Jesus Christ.

Jesus says "I am." That's like saying "I myself, and only I, am." These are the same words God speaks to Moses way back in Exodus 3:6 when He declares, "I am the God of Abraham, and the God of Isaac, and the God of Jacob." Jesus says that "before Abraham was, I am" (Jhn. 8:58). Jesus is making it very clear that He is God, the second member of the Holy Trinity. When Jesus says "I am" there is power in that proclamation. As the soldiers come to arrest Him on the night of His betrayal, they state that they are looking for Jesus of Nazareth and Jesus responds, "I am he" (Jhn. 18:5). So powerful was this proclamation that those who came to do Jesus harm, fell to the ground (Jhn. 18:6).

St. Peter echoes Jesus' words, "I am the way" in his defense before the elders of the Temple in the 4th chapter of the book of Acts. Peter and John had offered a lame man that which they had, the life-healing power of Jesus Christ (Acts 3:6). The lame man didn't just walk; he walked and leaped and praised God. St. Peter then challenged all who had witnessed this miracle to "repent, so that times of refreshing may come from the presence of the Lord" (Acts 3:19). The leaders are upset by all this and arrest St. John and St. Peter. When asked to explain himself, St. Peter makes clear "there is salvation in no one else, for there is no other name under heaven given among men by which we must be saved" (Acts 4:12).

When Jesus says "I am the truth" he is telling us that He is Truth. There is no other "truth", no alternative facts, no wiggle room for maybe, sort of truth. He is saying definitively that He is the only Truth.

Remember that Satan's lie in the Garden questioned God's truth and substituted an "alternative truth", a lie. Satan said if you eat the forbidden fruit, not only will you not die, but you will be like God. How often do we accept "alternative truth" only to later understand that just means untruth? Jesus declares Himself to be "the truth." The reality of existence is found only in Jesus Christ.

After telling His disciples that He was about to die, Jesus declared that He is "the life." Where death had come to mankind by Adam's sin, Jesus says that He is the life. Though He will die, He will take his life up again (ff Jn 10:14). And then He describes what life in Christ is really all about, "because I live, you will live also. In that day you will know that I am in my Father, and you in me, and I in you" (Jhn. 14:19b -20). Jesus is proclaiming that He is the very God of Creation, the Lord who blessed Abraham, and the Holy One who inhabits eternity. He is saying that those who are alive in Christ are in communion with, are in relationship with, are one with the Father in and through Christ Jesus! Where the sin of Adam broke that intimate walk with God, Jesus restores communion in and through Himself, Emmanuel, God with us.

As the new Adam, Jesus is making all things anew. St. Paul tells us that God has, "made known to us in all wisdom and insight the mystery of his will, according to his purpose which he set forth in Christ as a plan for the fulness of time, to unite all things in him, things in heaven and things on earth"(Eph. 1:9b-10). The phrase t"o unite"is translated from the Greek term α ţεφαʒαŢώ α şαŢ (anakephalaiōsasthai; in Latin, recapitulare, to recapitulate). It is in this recapitulation that Jesus has come to redeem and restore what God had intended, which was lost and broken because of Adam's sin in the Garden of Eden.

We do well to remember that all of creation was affected by Adam's sin. Not just mankind, but the totality of creation was disordered. It cannot be otherwise. Adam was instructed to have dominion over all of creation. When he sinned, that right ordering was lost. We experience the effects of this dis-ordering every day! The wolf and the lamb no longer lived in peaceful harmony. The soil no longer produced a bountiful supply of food. Men would no longer live in peace with God, rather fear was now the norm. No longer would mankind work together as partners in the tasks God had given, but rather, competition, jealousy, and distrust would rule.

The truth is that all of creation longs to "be set free from its bondage to decay" (Rom. 8:22). If we go all the way back to that fateful moment in the Garden of Eden when God confronts Adam and Eve after their sin, we see the results of that sin and its effect on all creation; "cursed is the ground because of you" (Gen. 3:17). St. Paul speaks of the "futility" creation is subjected to because of man's sin. What a trainwreck! One act of disobedience brought disorder, brokenness, and futility to all of creation. How can this be so?

When God created the heavens and the earth, everything He had made was "very good" (Gen 1.31). This is the condition of all creation, very good. The Hebrew word for good is *tob* which expresses the ideas of moral goodness (Genesis 2:17; Psalm 37:27), fruitfulness (Genesis 41:22), abundance (Judges 8:32), as well as pleasing in an aesthetic sense (Esther 1:11). This describes all of God's creation before the Fall.

Remember that abundance is primarily about relationship. All that is in proper relationship, or expressed another way, when all is in order with God, that is abundance. It is the abundance experienced in the Garden of Eden before the Fall. Scripture tells us that after the Fall of man the ground was cursed (Gen. 3.17) and that the beginning of new life, (childbirth) would be with great pain.

It is here we see the first effects of sin, and ultimately, the whole of creation experiences the decay and corruption of sin. Ultimately, all of creation is either under the law of sin and death which is futility and decay in the words of St. Paul, or it is under the "law of the Spirit of life in Christ Jesus" (Rom. 8:2), which is "life, and that more abundantly". There is no third option. Adam's sin brought futility and decay to all creation.

Consider for a moment the opening words of the Gospel of St. John,

> In the beginning was the Word, and the Word was with God, and the Word was God. He was in the beginning with God; all things were made through him, and without him was not anything made that was made. In him was life, and the life was the light of men. (John 1:1-4)

The opening phrase takes us back to Creation, "In the beginning . . ." and reminds us that it is the ever-present God who is the life of all. The sinful fall of man separated not only mankind but all of creation from the life that is only in God. This is what St. Paul is speaking of in the first chapter of his letter to the Colossians. "In him (Christ Jesus) all things hold together." Or stated negatively, apart from him (Christ Jesus) all things fall apart. And it is clear that everything is broken, it has all fallen apart. All of "creation waits with eager longing for the revealing of the sons of God" (Rom. 8:19). This is when the curse will be lifted and the intimate bond, the perfect fellowship of God the Creator and His creation is finally and fully restored. At the moment of Christ's victory over the last foe to be defeated, death; hope was renewed for all creation. The promise is that one day soon "there shall be no more anything accursed" (Rev. 22:3) and that "creation itself will be set free from its bondage to decay" (Rom. 8:21).

This restoration of what had been before the Fall is possible only because of the "new Adam." In 1 Corinthians 15:45, St. Paul compares Jesus to Adam: "Thus it is written, 'The first man Adam became a living being'; the last Adam became a life-giving spirit." The first Adam, created by God from the dust of the earth disobeyed and broke communion with God, and as we have seen, truly broke all of creation. The first Adam's sin spread sin and death to all mankind (See Rom. 5:12). No one escapes the curse. Scripture goes so far as to tell us, "none is righteous, no, not one" (Rom. 3:9). Even more clearly, even apart from the stain of original sin, St. Paul declares a little later in the same passage, "all have sinned and fall short of the glory of God" (Rom. 3:23). This sinfulness is death!

The last Adam, Christ Jesus, comes to redeem and restore fallen man and all creation. While the first Adam's disobedience brought brokenness, despair, and the reign of death (Rom. 5:17); the last Adam brought the abundant grace of God that brings salvation, justification, and righteousness. Adam, by the act of original pride of self, of arrogance disobedience brought death, and destruction. Adam's sin introduced inordinate desires and spiritual blindness. Christ, the new Adam, by His perfect obedience to the will of the Father restored man to his original communion with God, the source of life. This communion, only in and through Christ the new Adam has opened the gate to Paradise and life eternal in God's presence.

All of this to restore what was lost in the Fall. All of this to again bring mankind back into the image and likeness of our Creator. Those who love God, those who obey God, are being "conformed to the image of his Son" (Rom. 8:29). This conforming to the image of Christ is the secret of life in Christ, it is also the great challenge of life in Christ. St. Paul encourages the Corinthians (and us!) that, in Christ, we are a new creation (2 Cor. 5:17). The Last Adam, Christ, has restored us as adopted sons and daughters of God to share in His divine life!

Remember that God's plan from the very beginning is for mankind, His prize creation, to share in His own blessed life (CCC 1). God never intended for there to be sickness and death. He never intended for there to be brokenness and hurt. It was not His will that mankind should turn from Him in rebellion and self-trust. Never did He want there to be pain in childbearing or "sweat of the brow work" to eke out an existence. God has intended from the very beginning to share His blessed life with mankind.

He always intended for you and I to share in the abundance of life in Him. While He never intended these things, He was not surprised by them. His plan was not thwarted by the wickedness of Satan or of fallen man. Rather, in infinite love and mercy, God set in motion His plan of redemption and reconciliation to draw man back to Himself and renew the face of the earth.

His plan is the embodiment of the law of the Spirit of life in Christ Jesus. By the incarnation of the one and only begotten Son of God, God offered a new creative act. This would come through the One who didn't consider "equality with God as something to be grasped" (Phil. 2:6). Adam and Eve had grasped at being "like God." Satan had enticed them with that sweet-sounding promise of being like God. The old Adam was all about being one's own god.

In the words of St. Irenaeus, "The Word ... by whom all things were made, in the fullness of time, to recapitulate and contain all things became man in order to destroy death, to manifest life, and to restore the union between God and man" (St. Irenaeus, Epideixis, translated in Mersch, The Whole Christ, Milwaukee, 1938, p. 232). In this new union between God and man, life is restored to the living dead. Those apart from God are dead in their sin, though there is still breath in the lungs. Separation from God is death. Period. No if, or ands, or buts. To be separated from God by sin, is death. Remember the words of St. Paul in his letter to the Romans, "the wages of sin is death."

Separated from God by sin is to live in a disordered reality, a temporally centered reality that denies the spiritual realm, and with that, denies the realm of God, the life in Christ that is eternal. For St. Paul continues in his letter to the Romans, "the free gift of God is eternal life in Christ Jesus our Lord" (Rom. 6:23).

Section 3 Heaven on Earth?

Whom have I in heaven but you? And there is nothing on earth that I desire besides you. (Ps. 73:25)

Chapter 9

The Kingdom is Here, but Not Yet!

Thy kingdom come. Thy will be done, On earth as it is in heaven.
(Matt 6:10)

The question is pressing. It hangs as heavy in the air as the dew of the morning, if Jesus has made all things new, if creation has been recapitulated, if God's intended order has been restored, why are we not seeing Paradiso right now? After all, didn't Jesus cry out "It is finished" as He hung on the cross? Isn't the work of restoring communion with God done? So, shouldn't the fruits of that be completely and fully evident? While that would seem to be the case, we experientially know it is not.

With the prefigurements of the Old Testament in mind, the story of God's deliverance of His chosen people from Egypt is instructive. Remember that the Children of Israel had lived in Egypt for 400 years. First, they came as honored guests (see Genesis 37 – 50). Joseph, the son of Jacob, had been sold into slavery by his own brothers. God had a plan to restore Jacob's family, and Joseph would be instrumental in that plan.

Joseph marshaled the resources of Egypt during a time of plenty to provide bread enough for not only Egypt but also his own family. The famine, though harsh, brought Joseph's family back together. They lived in an area of Egypt called Goshen. While still a part of Egypt, it was removed enough from the center of Egyptian life that the Children of Israel were able to live, grow and multiply pretty much undisturbed. Until a new pharaoh came on the scene, one that did not know Joseph.

This pharaoh enslaved the Children of Israel. He increased the workload demanded of them. He slaughtered the male children of the Israelites. Then God sent one to lead His Chosen People back to the land of Promise, the land of abundance, the land promised to Abraham, Isaac, and Jacob (see Exodus 1 – 13). After the plague of the death angel, the night when the angel of death passed over the homes that had the blood of a lamb, properly prepared and consumed, spread on the doorposts. . . the Passover, God led His people out of Egypt.

He led them through the waters of the Red Sea. They passed through on dry land as God delivered them from the slavery of Egypt. He would lead them by a pillar of fire by night and a cloud by day. They would pass through the wilderness, arrive at the mountain of God (Sinai), receive the nation-making covenant (the Mosaic Covenant), and arrive at the edge of the Promised Land.

The Promised Land is the earthly home of God's Chosen People. It is a land of abundance, flowing with milk and honey. They are to go in and possess the land. They are to establish a nation of priests for all the nations. But it will require discipline. It will require faith in God and submission to His will and way. It will require effort. The current inhabitants of the land must be removed. No compromise is to be made. There is to be no accommodation with the Canaanites.

You may be wondering why we are considering this recitation of the Exodus of God's people. Remember that "in the Old Testament the New is concealed, in the New the Old is revealed" (St. Augustine). When we look at the typology of the Old Testament, we can see slavery in Egypt as representing slavery to the gods of this world and the resulting slavery to sin. This is why God says, "I am the LORD your God, who brought you out of the land of Egypt, out of the house of bondage (Ex. 20:2). The house of bondage, slaves to sin. Even as God provides daily bread, (manna from heaven), causes water to flow from, and guides them through a desolate wilderness, the Israelites return to the gods of Egypt.

This is what is happening at the foot of Mt. Sinai when they make a golden calf and engage in what Exodus 32:6 euphemistically calls "play." The golden calf (probably a representation of the Egyptian god, Apis) is worshipped with sacrifices and even a shared meal. The "play" is the kind of non-marital sexual activity that was associated with much pagan worship. From idolatry to adultery in one moment. No wonder Moses was so angry when he came down from the mountain!

These same people would arrive at the border of the Promised Land and lament that they were not still slaves in Egypt. (See Numbers 14). They still had not learned what it means to walk in communion with God. So, back to the wilderness, 40 years in the wilderness, until every person over the age of 20 has died. Fast forward to the moment that the Children of Israel, under the leadership of Joshua, (which by the way is translated in Greek to be Jesus), enter the Promised Land. While on one level the Promised Land is a prefigurement of heaven, it is more fundamentally a prefigurement of our earthly walk with Christ.

The Israelites still had to defeat the Canaanites. They were instructed to "utterly destroy" the inhabitants of the land, (Duet. 20:17-18). This was to be done for a very specific reason. It was too easy to learn the ways of foreign gods. It was too easy to be swayed by the visual in place of the invisible. It had happened before; it would happen again . . . and again . . . and again.

Even though they had battles to fight, and inhabitants to defeat; the Promised Land was theirs already, just not yet. So, it is for us as God's new Israel. We are already reigning with Him as His children, and yet that reign is not yet fully realized, in our lives, or in the world at large. The temptations of this world are far too real, their siren song not much different from the words of the serpent in the Garden when he intoned "Did God really say?" and "You will not die." And that leads us to our next question.

Chapter 10

If Everything is New, Why Do the Weeds Grow so Quickly?

For whatever a man sows, that he will also reap. (Gal 6:7)

The worst part of gardening for me is dealing with the weeds! They grow faster, stronger, taller, better rooted, and so on and so on . . . We work hard to lay the garden out just so. We till the soil. We start seedlings. We wait till the weather is just right and then we plant! With excitement and anticipation of the harvest, we plant a garden. And the harsh reality of the curse of Genesis takes over. "Cursed is the ground because of you; in toil, you shall eat of it all the days of your life; thorns and thistles it shall bring forth to you" (Gen. 3:17b -18a). I don't know about you, but I can grow a great crop of thorns and thistles!

A few years ago, we toured a series of farms in Boulder, Colorado. One farm was an organic farm: no weed killers, no artificial fertilizers. It was with great interest I heard the owner of the organic farm admit that some years the weeds overran the crops. That field was lost for the year. Sounds like our lives. Sometimes the weeds of sin threaten to overrun the work of life in Christ Jesus that God has started in us. We must return to pulling weeds over and over. The dandelions seem to always outproduce daisies.

Sin is a bit like a dandelion. The dandelion is primed for survival and proliferation. My grandfather often said that the dandelions in the yard had roots in . . ., well, you know! The seed globe sends forth its seeds at the slightest breeze.. And somehow, those seeds are quick to take root and sprout as new plants with roots in . . ., well, you know! Sin does that to our souls. Its roots are deep within us. Sin multiplies in our lives at an incredible rate. Did you ever tell a "little" lie, and then had to tell many more to cover that one "little" lie? That's the way sin works. A little goes a long way. In the words of a song, "Sin will take you farther than you want to go."

We really don't like to talk about sin. In fact, sin may be among the least understood concepts of life. I say this because we can identify certain actions that we call sin. But we really need to expand our understanding of sin considering what the Church teaches us.

The rooting out of the dandelions, the sins, those offenses against "reason, truth, and right conscience" (CCC 1849) is the work of conversion. Our continued actions "contrary to the eternal law" put us in the Garden alongside Eve as she acts in disbelief, distrust, and disobedience against God Himself.

St. Pope John Paul II says, "Conversion requires convincing of sin; it includes the interior judgment of the conscience, and this, being a proof of the action of the Spirit of truth in man's inmost being, becomes at the same time a new beginning of the bestowal of grace and love: "Receive the Holy Spirit." (John Paul II, *Dominum et Vivificantem* 31). It is walking in this new beginning, walking in the Way that is Christ, that defeats, bit by bit, the evil we do in God's sight (See Ps. 52:4).

Here's the crux of the matter, the stain of original sin is washed clean in the waters of baptism. The evil one is defeated in our lives, but we still struggle with a deep-seated bent toward sin. The Catechism calls this concupiscence an inclination to evil (CCC 405), and an inclination to sin (CCC 418). Here we see *already, but not yet* at its clearest. We are already holy, but not yet holy. We are already of the world that is to come, but still in this world. We are freed from original sin and turned back "towards God, but the consequences for nature, weakened and inclined to evil, persist in man and summon him to spiritual battle (CCC 405).

The dandelions grow so quickly because this "inclination to sin" is a powerful enemy. Indeed, it is called "the tinder for sin" because it is so easy for the smallest spark of sin to turn into a complete life-destroying conflagration. Unchecked, concupiscence will lead us away from fidelity to God to our own deluded self-dependence. Adam certainly did not fully comprehend where his act of prideful disobedience would lead him and all that would come after him. He ignored the still small voice of his conscience, choosing rather to believe the lie of all lies.

Adam could not have imagined the substantive change that would now be the basis of his very existence. That change was a break from reality. Up until that moment of sin, Adam lived and existed in perfect communion and relationship with God and the reality that is, because God is. In Adam's newly disordered existence, his experience of "reality" was a far cry from God's intention.

This disordered existence was blind to the fidelity, abundance, and intimacy, of walking with God. Rather in this new pseudo-reality, Adam thought himself to be the master of his own soul and destiny. The natural inclination and desire of his heart for God was blinded and dead to that for which he was created. From that moment, man's primary focus was on himself and the desires of his disordered reality. No longer could Adam serve as God's prophet, priest, or king. Dominion over creation was surrendered to the lie of the serpent and the disordered reality that lie brought. Only then did Adam begin to understand the awful loneliness of broken communion with God. Only then did the shame of his nakedness become real. Only then did the complete subjection of mankind's very nature to the darkness of sin become evident.

That change, the fundamental change from children of the light, children of God the Most High, to children of darkness, blind and lost, apart from their Creator, away from the only One in whom the fullness of existence can be found, is the change that St. Paul calls being "slaves of sin" (Rom. 6:17). No longer free in the sonship of God, but subject to the "law of sin and death" (Rom. 8:2). No longer capable of walking with God, but rather naturally inclined to walk after the flesh (Rom. 8:1 ff).

Through the waters of Baptism, the sacramental grace is given that cleanses us from original sin, and any sin that we have committed (See CCC 978). St. Paul tells us that we are buried into death with Christ by baptism and raised "by the glory of the Father" so that we "might walk in the newness of life" (Rom. 6:4). This "walk in the newness of life" is the Christian's life in Christ lived on earth.

Like the Promised Land of the Children of Israel, this new life is a life of abundance, flowing with milk and honey. The abundance is the deep, rich relationship with God through Christ. (It's not an abundance of *stuff*, for where our treasure is, there is also where our heart will be! Matt. 6:21).

Conversion, turning from the natural inclination to walk after the flesh will require discipline. It will require faith in God and submission to His will and way. It will require effort. The current habits of sin must be removed. No compromise is to be made. There is to be no accommodation with the flesh. Our entire life must be turned toward God, only here will we find the joy and happiness that is ours in Christ.

And here it is, this is why the dandelions grow so quickly! We are creatures bent towards the old fleshly, sinful nature. We are saved, but not yet. We are still in the struggle "against the impulses of concupiscence, which constantly tempts us to the commission of sin" (The Roman Catechism, Article 10). Our original nature, untested by temptation and unencumbered by sin and in a state of original holiness and justice, would have been at worst ambivalent towards sin, and most properly, absolutely opposed to sin. Adam and Eve were properly ordered toward God before the Fall. But because of the Fall, that proper ordering has been broken. The soul has been wounded, even unto death. For outside of the redeeming, life-giving salvation in Christ, we are dead men walking. But through the sacrament of baptism, "you were washed, you were sanctified, you were justified in the name of the Lord Jesus Christ and in the Spirit of our God" (1 Cor. 6:11). We are made participants in the life of Christ (Rom. 6:3-4)!

Except for one tiny little detail that explains so very much of our ongoing battle with sin; "Baptism, by imparting the life of Christ's grace, erases original sin and turns a man back toward God but the consequences for nature, weakened and inclined to evil, persist in man and summon him to spiritual battle" (CCC 405). There it is again, the wounded, broken, disordered condition of our very being, though healed in Christ, is not yet heaven-ready. Though turned back toward God; for this is what repentance really means, to turn from sin to God, not yet fully converted into a sin-free child of God. This is why we speak of continuing conversion. When we are baptized, we make certain promises or vows. These include a profession of faith made in response to a series of questions. This profession is basically a recitation of the Creed and follows questions about our relationship with Satan and sin:

V. Do you renounce sin,
so as to live in the freedom of the children of God?
R. I do.

V. Do you renounce the lure of evil,
so that sin may have no mastery over you?
R. I do.

V. Do you renounce Satan,
the author and prince of sin?
R. I do.

The challenge of the Christian life is to live in the freedom of the children of God when the lure of evil and the mastery of sin over us is so very strong. The Roman Catechism even states that "there is scarcely one to be found among us, who opposes so vigorous a resistance to its (concupiscence) assaults, or who guards his salvation so vigilantly, as to escape all wounds" (The Roman Catechism, Article 10).

In the garden of our lives, both literal and figurative, we are constantly summoned to the battle against the weeds that will destroy the very life we so desperately want. The weeds are always threatening to choke out life before life even has a chance to flourish.

Chapter 11

Concupiscence, Concupiscence, Concupiscence, the Triple Threat

For all that is in the world, the lust of the flesh and the lust of the eyes and the pride of life, is not of the Father but is of the world.
(1 John 2:16)

If you get the feeling that concupiscence is a problem, consider triple concupiscence for a moment. St. John, in his first letter, speaks of this triple concupiscence. "All that is in the world" can be summed up in three variations or strains of concupiscence. These are the same three great temptations that Christ faced in the wilderness. And even more to the point, these are the very temptations that Satan confronted Eve with all the way back in the Garden of Eden.

All of these come from the disordering of reality that occurs when we ignore God and His intentions, His plan, His perfection and seek our own. Remember that when God created, He declared, "it is good", and when God created man, He declared "it is very good!" But, tempted by Satan, led into distrust and disobedience, man wanted more. He wanted to be like God. This is the lie of concupiscence, that somehow, our surrender to these temptations will open to us the "good" things that God doesn't want us to have, including being like God himself!

A close reading of the story of the Fall in Genesis 3 illuminates each of these as part of the lie of Satan and the response of the heart that distrusts God. After twisting what God said, the serpent listened to Eve's reiteration of what God had decreed, "You shall not eat of the fruit of the tree, which is in the midst of the garden, neither shall you touch it, lest you die" (Gen. 3:3). Then the serpent hit Eve right where we humans are the most vulnerable, always wanting more, always wanting to be in charge, always wanting to be the final authority for self.

The serpent says, "You will not die . . .you will be like God (Gen. 3:4, 5). What powerfully enticing words, "you will be like God." What a promise! Except it is a lie. We all know that if something is too good to be true, it's not. This lie was, and is, simply too good to be true!

Before Eve ate of the forbidden fruit, before Adam joined her in their pursuit of being like God, they were the children of God! They lived in His Garden, walking and talking with Him. They were being all that God had created them to be. Yet they bought the lie. And we follow their lead every time we decide to go our own way! Every time we allow the bent toward sin to control our thoughts and decisions, our actions take us away from home. Away from the Father. Away from our greatest, and most powerful actualization. We become like the son who took his inheritance and left. (See Luke 15.)

We are sure that we can make life better on our own. Except we can't. Like that son, all we can see is the immediate gratification of self. Like that son, all we can see is the "good" things of the world. Like that son, all we want is to be our own boss, our own person. It may work for a short time, but make no mistake, the end is death.

This triple concupiscence, the lust of the flesh, the lust of the eyes, and the pride of life constantly challenge our mastery of self. Overcoming concupiscence will require a reordering of self, reordering according to God's way. We can never forget that "There is a way which seems right to a man, but its end is the way to death" (Pro. 16:25).

The Lust of the Flesh

It seems odd that the fruits and vegetables in the produce section of the local grocer often look so much better than the ones that I grow in my garden! (I think mine almost always tastes better!) Turns out the grocer only offers Grade 1, and in my garden, I grow all grades! Produce is graded on freshness, visual defect, color, size, and overall quality that affects flavor. In other words, it must look good! Genesis says that all the fruits and vegetables looked good and tasted good. Plus, there was an abundance of it all. This is related to us when we read that the Eve saw that the forbidden fruit was "good for food." The lust of the flesh is concerned about the body.

Yes, it includes sexual gratification. Yes, it includes gluttony. Yes, it includes any gratuitous seeking of pleasure. St. Paul speaks of the "passions of our flesh" (Eph. 2.3). Flesh is used not in the sense of skin and bones, but rather, about the human nature that is opposed to God. In the disordered world of "fleshly passions", we are inclined to take whatever we want, whatever satisfies our own interests, pleasure, and fulfillment. The lust of the flesh is any of the wicked desires stirred by our physical or emotional needs, particularly the desire for pleasures.

It seems that the pursuit of any pleasure, in any form, is now normal and accepted in almost every area of society. St. Paul warned it would be so in his second letter to St. Timothy that in the last days, men would love pleasure more than they would love God (2 Tim. 3.4). Virtually every facet of social media promotes uninhibited, gratuitous pleasure as the secret to a happy, fun, fulfilled life. The problem is that what looks "good for food" is actually death for the soul.

Most of the time, this disordered pursuit of pleasure comes at a cost to someone else. It is based on taking what I want. This stands in stark contrast to the love of God that gives. The very love that we are called to live in. Eve couldn't see the abundance that God had provided, only what she wanted in that moment. Sound familiar? Appetite is a dangerous thing to surrender control to.

The Lust of the Eyes

Have you ever seen something and in that instant, you just knew you had to have it? Maybe a new car, that new 85-inch TV, or maybe something even more insidious? Welcome to the lust of the eyes! The lust of the eyes can best be described as

the sinful desire to want to have the things we see, such as money, possessions, houses, cars, a certain physical appearance, or even looking at someone lustfully.

Yep, pornography, salacious TV shows, fantasies, other's possessions; these are all lust of the eyes. Eve looked at the forbidden fruit and "it was a delight to the eyes." How often we see things and are delighted to the point of wanting, scheming, plotting to find a way to claim the delightful thing as our own.

The eyes can be such a portal for sin to overtake us. When I was a child, cereal companies enticed us to buy their brand by offering very exciting, great looking rewards. One brand offered an airplane. Send in enough box tops and receive a Cessna model airplane. Man, that airplane looked great on the side of that cereal box. I could see it in my hand. I could see me flying it around the house. Maybe even making my brother wish he had one! When the plane finally arrived, reality slapped me in the face. The fabulous prize was just a little plastic plane less than 3 inches long! It wasn't at all what had grabbed my eye! My brother laughed at what I had so longed for.

That is what the lust of the eyes always does, it looks so good, you can't refuse it, you must have it! And then, it shows its true self, death! Fantasy is just that, fantasy. I can watch Lifestyles of the Rich and Famous over and over and dream/ fantasize about that being me! I can imagine what I would do with the winnings from the lottery! Just more lust of the eyes. The eyes can be a powerful force in our lives.

The Pride of Life

The "pride of life" is a life that is lived in opposition to God and his commands. It is an autonomous life, a life where we think we have no need of God. Sometimes I jokingly declare that there are only two ways to do something, "my way, or the wrong way." When we take such thoughts seriously, we are living in the pride of life.

My way is the wrong way. My way insists that it is right, at least for me. This is why so many people today say things like, "this is my truth." What a foolish position! Truth is not adaptable for each individual. Truth is truth. When I demand that "my truth" is right at least for me, we have displaced God as the King of the universe. We have set ourselves as the ruler of our universe. In that place we demand that others acknowledge and accept our truth, and Satan dances with glee! Why? Because This attitude declares that I have the right to live any way I want, without reference to the One in whose image I am made, without regard to any consequences outside of self. Pride of life is the temptation and desire for power, personal recognition, and personal glory. Pride of life appeals to arrogance, conceitedness, and narcissism.

Christ and Triple Concupiscence

When we consider the ongoing effect of Adam and Eve's decision to disobey God and go their own way, we can feel a little overwhelmed and unprepared for this battle of the soul. After all, the power of concupiscence explains so much about the darkness, the evil, the disorder of our world. Who can bear up against this seemingly overwhelming tide?

Remember that the old Roman Catechism says that rare is the one who fights so successfully against concupiscence that he is never wounded by sin. So, since we are all sinners, since we are all subjected to, and given to concupiscence, where do we find hope? Where do we find the way to overcome the sinful passions of the flesh? How do we follow St. Paul's exhortation to "not gratify the desires of the flesh" (Gal. 5:16).

Let us consider Jesus Christ. The author of Hebrews tells us that Jesus is the "one who in every respect has been tempted as we are, yet without sinning" (Heb. 4:15). Jesus, the Son of God, born of the Virgin Mary has been tempted and tested in every way that you and I are!

In other words, while without original sin, while blameless, Christ was tempted and tested in all the ways that you and I can be in regard to divine commands.

You see Adam and Eve were tempted (and succumbed) to violate God's command, His will. It is from this rejection of the Divine will that all sinfulness flows. It is from this violation of God's will that death, the enemy of life overshadows and overwhelms life. It is from this violation of the Word of God.

So, the question isn't whether Jesus was tempted to view pornography on his mobile device, it's not that he fights every conceivable human urge, it's that he is tempted in the three major areas of human vulnerability. The three foundational forms of concupiscence. The desire to live in the works of the flesh, "immorality, impurity, licentiousness, idolatry, sorcery, enmity, strife, jealousy, anger, selfishness, dissension, party spirit, envy, drunkenness, carousing (Gal. 5: 19) all come from the primary sin, which is to act contrary to God.

Adam, up until the fall was in a state of original holiness. Adam was without sin and without the attendant disordered desires and priorities that are the result of sin. (This is, at least partly, why Adam and Eve are naked before the Fall without shame.) Once Adam rejected God's Word, all of man's existence was plunged into the depths of brokenness and disorder. Nothing was as it was intended to be. The desires of the flesh multiplied and grew to dominate the very existence of mankind. (Check out the results in Gensis 6!)

The question is, will Jesus, the last Adam, do the will of the One who sent Him? Will the last Adam, Jesus, reject the wooing of Satan and his invitation to disobedience and self?

Will Jesus remain true to the task for which He was sent? The first Adam had rejected sonship for self-ship.

The last Adam is the Son, will He reject His very being, His very Essence to satisfy self? Just as the first Adam was tempted to reject God's Word, the last Adam was also tempted to reject the word and will of God.

We read of this tempting in the synoptic Gospels. Several things stand out as we read of this episode in Jesus' life. First, we notice that at the baptism of Jesus, The Father declares, "This is my beloved Son, with whom I am well pleased" (Matt. 3:17). Compare this with how God responded when He has created Adam, "it was very good." Now His Son, His one and only Son, the Lamb of God has come, and He is well pleased!

When Adam is tempted, all he had ever experienced was the abundance of God. All that he needed for life, in all its fullness, was provided. There was no greater happiness available to him than his communion with God, the Father. Adam works in the Garden; he names the animals. The lion that plays with the little lamb. All the animals are docile. There are no wild beasts, there is abundant food. Water freely flows to water the Garden and the world beyond. It is the lush, abundant temple of God. And God is there.

After Jesus is baptized, he is led by the Spirit into the wilderness. Led by the Spirit to the wilderness. Why? Let us remember that Jesus has come to redeem and restore all that has been lost because of Adam's sin. The Garden is left a barren wilderness because of Adam's sin. The once docile animals have become wild beasts. The waters no longer flow. Life is a constant struggle for survival in this arid, sterile place.

So, led by the Spirit, Jesus enters the wilderness, the symbol of the cursedness and barrenness of the fallen world.

He is there with the wild beasts and is unharmed. He is not trapped and deceived by Satan, but rather, is the Son who does the will of the Father.

For forty days, much like the 40 years that the children of Israel wander in the wilderness, Jesus is alone fasting in the wilderness. Unlike the Children of Israel, we do not read of His murmuring or complaining about His time in the wilderness. Unlike Adam and Eve, who never experienced hunger, He is hungry. It is in this moment of hunger that Satan comes to tempt Jesus.

The lust of the flesh is the first temptation. "If you are the Son of God, command these stones to become loaves of bread" (Matt. 4:3). Just as Eve saw that the fruit was good for food, for the meeting of the fleshly desires, Jesus is challenged to satisfy his physical desires.

Satan seems to always know just how to attack! In the Garden, he misquotes God (and so did Eve). Instead, Jesus responds by accurately quoting Sacred Scripture, "It is written, 'Man shall not live by bread alone, but by every word that proceeds from the mouth of God'" (Matt. 4:4). We should take notice that Jesus quotes from the book of Deuteronomy. This is the book that summarizes the lessons the Children of Israel learned during their forty years in the wilderness. It is a book that offers the covenantal blessing of God and the just punishment for rejecting God's covenant.

Jesus returns to the dependency on the abundant provision and sure direction of the word of God. (And of course, we Catholics feast abundantly on the living Word of God in the Holy Eucharist!) Jesus' response is a clear indication of what He repeats again and again, He has come to do His Father's will. How different from Eve's timid response to Satan, and her turning from the will of her Creator. It is from this same book that Jesus quotes in response to the next two temptations that Satan hurls at Christ.

Satan challenges Jesus to prove His divine Sonship by throwing himself from the pinnacle of the temple. In this temptation, Satan returns to his devious ways of misquoting what God says. Satan misquotes, takes from context, and misuses Psalm 91. (You really should read the Psalm, it is a series of beautiful promises of God's protection for those live in the protecting shelter of God, the Most High. Just think, if Satan would have quoted the next verse, he would have been quoting his own demise! ("The serpent you will trample under foot" Ps. 91:13b). And verse 14 is the real clincher, "Because he clings to me in love, I will deliver him." Jesus shuts Satan down by returning to God's will. By returning to God's word, "Again it is written, 'You shall not tempt the Lord your God'" (Matt. 4:7). Here Jesus quotes Deuteronomy 6:16. Moses is exhorting the Israelites to write the word of God on their hearts, to put it upon their doorposts. In that moment, Moses reminds the Children of Israel of their testing of God when they had no water in the wilderness. There God made water flow from the rock. (Compare that with Jesus' conversation with the woman at the well in John 4. Jesus offered living water, water that would spring up to eternal life! Jesus would not budge from obedience to the will of the Father.)

Finally, Satan offers Jesus everything, all the kingdoms of the world, the pride of life. Again, Satan asks Jesus to violate the word of God, to turn from the Divine will to human fulfillment. Remember that human fulfillment is always temporal, it just never lasts. All Jesus must do is fall down and worship Satan.

Let's not forget that Satan is a fallen angel. He and the demons "through themselves have become wicked."11 They are fallen exactly because they wanted to be equal with God. How self-aggrandizing to ask the Son of God to worship this fallen angel! And once again, Jesus returns to Deuteronomy and quotes, "'You shall worship the Lord your God and him only shall you serve.'"

Jesus makes it clear that He will only serve the Father. With that He does something powerful! "Begone Satan!" He orders the devil to leave! And he did! The result is the angels of God come and minster to Jesus!

The spirit led Jesus into the wilderness because Jesus was to take back, as the last Adam, what the first Adam lost. He did not go to be tempted. He went to take back what Satan had stolen. He went to succeed where Adam had failed. While there is a clear parallel in the temptation of Jesus to the areas of temptation that Adam and eve, and by extension, every one of us, the almighty god was never going to be subjugated to the devil.

The last Adam was the one "who, though he was in the form of God, did not count equality with God a thing to be grasped, but emptied himself, taking the form of a servant, being born in the likeness of men. And being found in human form he humbled himself and became obedient unto death, even death on a cross" (Phil. 2:6-8). Everything about Jesus' life and death was the antithesis of the triple concupiscence unleashed upon humanity by the deceit of Satan and the disobedience of Adam!

Jesus obeyed the Father. Jesus lived by, and as, the Word of the Father. In doing so, the last Adam made perfect use of His freedom. He freely chose to obey the Truth. He could declare that He was not only the Truth, but the Life and the Way. The way back to the life of communion with the Father. The way back to God's family. He is the One who, by His obedience, conquered the death, and hell, and the grave unleashed by the failure of the first Adam. He has overcome and offers to you and to me

---

[11] Henry Denzinger and Karl Rahner, eds., *The Sources of Catholic Dogma*, trans. Roy J. Deferrari (St. Louis, MO: B. Herder Book Co., 1954), 169.

that same victory, that same life, that same communion, that abundant life of restored relationship with God! Let's take a look at how we can be more fully alive in Christ by Christ living more fully in us.

Section 4

Gethsemane, the Garden of Choice

Realize that you must lead a dying life; the more a man dies to himself, the more he begins to live unto God. (THOMAS À KEMPIS)

Chapter 12

Prefiguring in the Journey to Gethsemane

The Bible is the story of two gardens. Eden and Gethsemane. In the first, Adam took a fall. In the second, Jesus took a stand.
(Max Lucado)

After the Last Supper, the Institution of the Eucharist and the Farewell Discourse, Jesus and his disciples took one final journey together. After they had sung a hymn, they headed out across through the Kidron Valley to the Mount of Olives. This was a familiar path for Jesus and the disciples. Just a short distance over the Mt. of Olives was the hamlet of Bethany. Bethany was the home of Jesus' friends Martha, Mary, and Lazarus.

The slopes of the Mt. of Olives were home to ancient Jewish cemeteries. The moonlight reflecting from the tombstones were undoubtably visible to Jesus, reminding Him of what was about to befall Him. Even Judas knew that Jesus often stopped in the olive tree garden on the slopes of the Mount of Olives. Scripture tells us that this was His custom! He went here often with His disciples. This garden, Gethsemane, or literally, *the olive press,* was a familiar place to Jesus. Apparently, he even had a particular place where He went to pray., St. Luke tells us, "When he came to the place. . ." (Lk. 22. 40). Jesus had done much this day to further the plan of God to reconcile all of creation through the last Adam. Let's look at some of the prefigurements that are realized in the event of this night.

First, and perhaps most obvious, is the prefiguring Passover of the Jewish people. The Last Supper is the fulfillment of the Passover meal from way back in Exodus when God was preparing to bring judgment on the land of Egypt. Remember that we said earlier that Egypt is a type or representation of the sinful world. But before God brings that just and right punishment, He first offers mercy. The children of Israel sacrificed a lamb, ate its flesh, drank the cup of blessing together, and placed the blood of the lamb on the doorposts of their home.

The night of the first Passover in Egypt, the mercy of God was provided to every home covered by the lamb's blood. Death was the judgement for sin, not just for Adam and Eve, but for all the households not covered by the lamb's blood. And yes, death is still the just and right judgment for sin that is not covered and cleansed by the Lamb's blood!

Jesus said he had earnestly desired to eat this meal with his disciples (See Lk 22:15). Why? Because the Passover meal is the retelling of God's deliverance of His people from Egypt. The Jews were required to relive this memorial each and every year! And now, Jesus, about to begin a new exodus, begins to set forth a new covenant, an eternal covenant. A covenant sealed with the precious outpoured blood of the Lamb of God slain from the foundations of the world!

This is the Lamb that God had told Abraham that would be provided, God Himself! All this to undo the terrible destruction and death because of sin in the Garden of Eden. And so, they share this most special meal, the Last Supper, together. The Last Supper, because no longer will the daily sacrifice of animals be required (see Heb. 7:27). No, He will offer up Himself, once, for all!

The Paschal meal, reconstituted as the Holy Eucharist, is the sign and seal of the new covenant. Jesus' Body and Blood is the new Manna from heaven. The survival of the children of Israel in the wilderness was dependent on the manna that was sent from heaven every day! Jesus called Himself "the Bread of Life from Heaven!" In the same discourse recorded in the 6th chapter of St. John's Gospel, Jesus also tells us that those who eat of this Bread will not die but will live forever (see John 6:30 – 59). There was much discussion and dispute among those gathered on the banks of the Sea of Galilee. Jesus settled, or perhaps defined, the dispute by declaring that "unless you eat the flesh of the Son of man and drink his blood, you have no life in you; he who eats my flesh and drinks my blood has eternal life, and I will raise him up at the last day" (Jhn. 6:53-54).

Now in the Upper Room, as He institutes the Holy Eucharist, Jesus clarifies exactly what He meant back on the seashore: His Body, His Blood, given for us the offspring of the first Adam are now brought into the family of God by the new covenant made and sealed with the Body and Blood of the last Adam. And He calls to not only his disciples in that room, but to whosoever will, "take, eat . . . drink of . . .my blood of the covenant, which is poured out for many for the forgiveness of sins" (Matt. 26:26-28). Remember when we looked at the five covenants God made with, Adam, Noah, Moses, Abraham, and David? Each of those covenants was a precursor to what was to come as God unveiled His plan to banish death and restore life to all who would receive His grace and mercy in Jesus Christ.

Jeremiah experienced the result of the long, complete rejection of God's covenants by His people. He suffered for his faithfulness to God. He witnessed the destruction of the Temple in Jerusalem as the Babylonians destroyed the city and took the Children of Israel captive. When it seemed that God had totally abandoned and turned his back on Israel, Jeremiah wrote these prophetic words of hope:

> Behold, the days are coming, says the LORD, when I will make a new covenant with the house of Israel and the house of Judah, not like the covenant which I made with their fathers when I took them by the hand to bring them out of the land of Egypt, my covenant which they broke, and I showed myself their Master, says the LORD. But this is the covenant which I will make with the house of Israel after those days, says the LORD: I will put my law within them, and I will write it upon their hearts; and I will be their God, and they shall be my people. And no longer shall each man teach his neighbor and each his brother, saying, 'Know the LORD,' for they shall all know me, from the least of them to the greatest, says the LORD; for I will forgive their iniquity, and I will remember their sin no more. (Jer. 31:31-34).

Did you read that? A new covenant! The law of God within, written on the heart. God will be their God, and they will be His people. And God will remember their sin no more! This is what Jesus is telling the disciples is now coming to reality! The new covenant, the one that God promised at the time of the destruction of the Temple, at the time of the end of the Israel as a viable nation, has now been made present!

No longer will God's children have hearts of stone. Hearts that submit to concupiscence in rebellion against God. No, now they will have a heart of flesh! A heart that is soft towards God. A heart that is filled with the Spirit of God. This is the New Covenant. This is brought to us in the Holy Eucharist, the Body and Blood, Soul, and Divinity of Jesus Christ. Wow! That's a lot going on in the Last Supper and Institution of the Eucharist! But wait! There's more!!!

After all of this has happened, Jesus gives what Scripture scholars often refer to as the Farewell Address. This address is found in chapters 13 – 17 of St. John's Gospel.

We might consider this a bookend to the Sermon on the Mount at the beginning of Jesus' earthly ministry. Much like prefiguring of Moses' farewell address that comprises most of the book of Deuteronomy, Jesus tells his disciples about what to expect as they enter the promised land of adoption as God's children. He warns them, He encourages them. He gives them instructions and offers them a new commandment. This commandment is the sign to all who see them. This commandment is the living out of the love He will demonstrate on Calvary's cross.

Perhaps most noticeable is that He offers them a view of God. Adam and Eve walked and talked with God face to face in the Garden of Eden. Now Jesus says that if you know Him, you know the Father; if you have seen Jesus, you have seen the Father! And then Jesus speaks of vines and branches. Of abiding in Him. Of being nothing apart from Him. And He speaks of tribulation. Of the certainty of tribulation. But not just tribulation. He offers peace. Peace in spite of and in the midst of tribulation.

He proclaims that He has overcome the world! The world of sin., The world of separation from God. The world of death and despair. And then He prays. (See John 17). Oh, how He prays. He prays for the disciples there with Him. He even prays for you and I and all who would come to believe through the words of the apostles! Finally, after all of this, the disciples follow Jesus out across the Kidron valley.

Passing across the valley floor, the pinnacle of the temple would have been visible. The temptation of Jesus and His victory over Satan easily recalled. The prophet Joel calls this the valley of decision (Joel 3:14). Decisions are to be made as they cross the valley and head to the Garden of Gethsemane. The prefigurement of crossing the Jordan, making the decision to follow Joshua into the land of promise is highlighted here as a new Joshua leads them forward.

There is still the work of taking the land back from those who are illegitimate squatters, usurping the land from its rightful inhabitants. We see this in the work that Jesus asks of the disciples as He asks them to pray to avoid temptation. Like the Children of Israel, they are not yet up to the task of repulsing the enemy. And so, Jesus reminds them "the spirit is indeed willing, but the flesh is weak" (Matt.26:41). Let us return to the Garden of Choice, Gethsemane.

Chapter 13

Gethsemane, the Olive Press

In Gethsemane the holiest of all petitioners prayed three times that a certain cup might pass from Him. It did not. (C. S. Lewis)

Gethsemane literally means olive press. Apparently, there were many such areas on the Mount of Olives. Olive oil was a precious commodity. Used for oil lamps, cooking, medicine, and most importantly, anointing, the oil of olives played an important role in the lives of the people. When the ripe olives were gathered, the fruit was placed in a huge stone basin. A large millstone was then rolled over the olives to grind and press the flesh to extract the precious oil. It is to this place that Jesus often came.

The Gospel of St. John speaks of Jesus entering the garden, leading some scholars to believe that this area was a walled garden, a special sanctuary of some wealthy benefactor. Regardless, it was a place well known to Jesus and the disciples. Even Judas knew it. It is here that the greatest battle yet will be fought. In this sanctuary, this special place. Much like the Garden of Eden. Much like the battle between the first Adam and Satan. Only now it is the last Adam, the Son of God who will do great battle. It is the Son of God whose obedience will be tested, and the fate of all mankind hangs in the balance.

Christ will be pressed and ground until the pure submission, the absolute obedience to the will of the Father is manifest. Yes, Jesus the man suffers the temptation to find another way. This was Peter's response to Jesus as Jesus explained the sufferings and death He would have to suffer. Peter rebuked Jesus and told Him that such things would never happen to the Christ. Jesus rebuked Peter, "Get behind me, Satan! You are a hindrance to me; for you are not on the side of God, but of men" (Matt. 16:21). And this is just shortly after Peter has declared that Jesus is the Christ! Peter is, in effect, saying that there is a different way, a way that does not include the Cross and its sufferings. A way that doesn't require death! A way that doesn't involve the shedding of the blood of an innocent Lamb. Peter has forgotten that "life is in the blood" and that man's way always ends in death, and that eternal.

Yes, Jesus must suffer. It is as it was prophesied. His heart is heavy, "very sorrowful, even to death" (Matt 26: 38). Jesus feels the loneliness of what is about to transpire. He feels the abandonment of the Father as He becomes sin for all mankind. He feels the depth of despair of death. He recognizes that His body will be bruised and broken. He will suffer the most degrading public humiliation, stripped naked just as the first Adam was naked. Beaten, mocked, derided. Spat upon. Accused of blaspheming His Father.

The Light of the world is plunged into the darkness of every sin ever committed and every sin that will ever be committed. The darkness and chaos of this moment is like the condition of the earth at the very beginning of creation, "The earth was without form and void, and darkness was upon the face of the deep" (Gen. 1:2). Just as the first Adam lost his sight of God when he sinned, Jesus too experiences the darkness of evil like no other has or ever will.

This is the weight upon Jesus in the Garden of Choice, the garden of the olive press, Gethsemane. The agony of it all is so intense that "his sweat became like great drops of blood falling down upon the ground" (Luke 22:44). Yet within all of that, Jesus is committed to the Father's will. He is willingly ready to be offered up on the altar of sacrifice, once, for all.

Remember when Abraham had brought Isaac to Mount Moriah to offer his son of promise, the one through whom God would make a way of reconciliation and redemption? Isaac was no small child, he went willingly. He obeyed his father to the point of sacrificing his own life. Let us not underestimate the intensity or weight of the choice that Jesus wrestled with as he prayed, "if it is possible, let this chalice pass from me" (Matt 22. 39; Luke 22:42). Nor should we think that Jesus has come to this moment to negotiate with God. He is not playing a game of "Let's Make a Deal."

No, Jesus is genuinely and fully bearing the sins, yes, yours and mine, of the whole world. In the words of St. Paul, "he humbled himself and became obedient unto death, even death on a cross" (Phil. 2:8). Jesus is suffering and at the same time becoming the model of surrender, of obedience to you and me. He is suffering the agony of the curse of sin that has haunted mankind since the Fall.

Recall that God told Eve that it would be in multiplied pain that she would birth children. And to Adam God said it would be with the sweat of his brow that bread would be eaten. In the Garden of Eden, the angels come to guard the Garden and keep mankind out. In the Garden of Gethsemane, they come to minister the obedient Son. The culmination of His prayer is "nevertheless, not my will but yours, be done" (Matt 26:39; Luke 22:42). The first Adam rebelled to become "like God." The first Adam would now live with the constant knowledge that from dust he had come, and to dust he would return, the soul sorrowfulness unto death was now a constant feature of man's existence. The last Adam,

> Though he was in the form of God, did not count equality with God a thing to be grasped, but emptied himself, taking the form of a servant, being born in the likeness of men. And being found in human form he humbled himself and became obedient unto death, even death on a cross. (Phil. 2:6-8)

Think deeply about those words. The last Adam was God and yet, He became a servant. A servant of the suffering, the sorrow, the separation. A Son who comes to the Father and does not demand His standing, but rather, obediently submits to death. Submits to death so that He might destroy death. That He might open the gate to Paradiso for all who will believe. To open the gates of Paradiso so there need be no more pain or suffering or separation! To open the gate to Paradiso, to redemption and reconciliation with the Father.

Hear the words of St. Paul, "as by one man's disobedience many were made sinners, so also by one Mans's obedience many will be made righteous" (Rom 5:19). St. Ambrose of Milan says, "the One that had no reason to sorrow for himself sorrowed for me, and leaving aside the enjoyment of his eternal divinity, he is afflicted with the weariness of my infirmity. He assumed my sadness, in order to confer on me his joy, and in our footsteps he descended even to the sorrow of death, in order to recall us to life in his own footsteps" (Commentary of Saint Ambrose on the Gospel According to Saint Luke).

The Letter to the Hebrews uses the phrase, "in the days of his flesh," an expression revealing Jesus' condition of human weakness that He willingly assumed so "that through death he might destroy him who had the power of death, that is, the devil" (Heb. 2:14). The author goes on to say, Jesus "learned obedience by the things which he suffered" paralleling the Gospel accounts in which Jesus, in his agony, submits his own will obediently to that of his Father (see Matt. 26:39,42; Mark 14:36; Luke 22:42).

These prayers in such agony and intensity are themselves sacrificial. Hebrews tells us that Jesus "offered" them. They are priestly prayers offered up to God. The Letter to the Hebrews tells us that these "prayers and supplications" of Jesus were heard on high because of his godly piety. Jesus' obedient reverence is exactly what we find as He prays in the Gospel accounts of the agony in Gethsemane.

How was Jesus "heard" when he offered up the prayers and supplications? Jesus prayed exactly in accordance with God's will. This is how he taught the disciples to pray, and this is how he prayed. St. John will teach us in his first letter, "Now this is the confidence that we have in him, that if we ask anything according to his will, he hears us" (1 John 5:14).

Because Christ was willing to humble himself to the Father's will that he, "having been perfected . . . became the author of eternal salvation to all who obey him" (Hebrews 5:9).
This was God's will, the will that Jesus prayed would be done. He was "made perfect through sufferings" (Heb. 2:10). It was because Jesus became obedient unto death that "God also has highly exalted him" (Phil. 2:9). In that moment, the moment of complete surrender, absolute trust in God, the Father, the angels of Heaven come and minster to Him.

Jesus prays in Gethsemane the same prayer He taught His disciples to pray; "thy will be done on earth as it is in heaven" (Matt. 6:10). Again, it is of interest that He finishes as He began. For the reference in St. Matthew's Gospel is from the Sermon on the Mount. In this early exposition of the Kingdom of God, the Kingdom Christ has come to establish on Earth, and in our hearts. He says, "Thy will be done on earth as it is in heaven." At the end of His earthly ministry, he cries out with the same refrain, "Thy will be done." This has been Jesus' refrain over and over during His earthly ministry. It is the purpose of His life!

The first Adam had the opportunity to do the will of the Father, to till and guard the Garden of Eden, but he traded it for a bite of forbidden fruit. He gave it away to be his own master. The last Adam says again and again, I have come to do the will of Him who sent me. What is the will of the Father? To bring salvation to the world, to redeem and restore all that was lost. To be the Prophet, Priest and King. In the Garden of Choice, Gethsemane, Jesus again chooses the will and way of the Father.

Some years ago, I had the opportunity to walk down the Palm Sunday path on the slopes of the Mount of Olives. This is where Jesus made his Triumphal Entry into the city.

The crowds cheered and cried, "Hosanna, blessed is He who comes in the name of the Lord." What a morning of excitement and anticipation that must have been. It certainly was for us pilgrims!

But just a few hours later our pilgrimage took us through the olive groves, to the Church of All Nations. This beautiful church is built on the site where tradition says Jesus prayed in Gethsemane. From the pinnacle of popularity to a place where even his closest disciples couldn't keep watch with him for an hour. It was a sobering experience.

This is where the Passion of our Lord began. This is where great drops of His blood were first shed. It was here that His obedience cost him his life. It was here that He modeled his teaching that "unless a grain of wheat falls into the earth and dies, it remains alone; but if it dies, it bears much fruit. He who loves his life loses it, and he who hates his life in this world will keep it for eternal life" (Jhn. 12:24-25). It was here that he revealed what is required for you and me to grow in the knowledge and image of our Lord. It is here in the Garden of Choice that we will fight the battle of our will and way versus God's will and way. It is in this Garden that we will feel the weight of the pressing stone as we surrender our will. It is here we will choose life or death, and that eternal.

Chapter 14

My Way or the High Way

For what is a man, what has he got, if not himself, then he has naught, To say the things he truly feels, And not the words of one who kneels. But more, much more than this I did it my way!
(Paul Anka)

Have you ever done a "trust" walk? You are blindfolded and must trust your partner to lead you safely on a walk? Or perhaps the "trust" fall, you are required to lean back until you fall backwards into (hopefully) the arms of your partner? Trust is a hard thing. After all, who can you really trust to have your best interests in mind?

The choice for both the first and the last Adam was my way or God's way. We know how that turned out. One brought death, the other life. Adam and Eve doubted God. They doubted His word. They doubted that communion with God, that walking and talking with the Creator would bring fulfillment and happiness. Pope Benedict XVI speaks of the mistrust sown by doubt. The Catechism of the Catholic Church speaks of man's trust in God dying in man's heart. The lie of the serpent causes doubt about living according to God's commandments, according to God's will. The serpent's "promise" is that you can be like God, you can do it your way, without kneeling down, free and finding ultimate fulfillment.

In the words of St. Maximus the Confessor, we want to be like God, but "without God, before God, and not in accordance with God." And isn't this the very substance of what sin really is, putting myself in God's place? In that place we make the decisions, take the actions that are going to bring me satisfaction, that in myself I have the power to be satisfied and happy! And yet we existentially know that the serpent's lie is simply not the truth. Everywhere we look, people are trying to find happiness, fulfillment, and meaning in their efforts, their possessions, their personal pleasure. Sounds just like what St. Paul warned in his second letter to St. Timothy:

> Men will be lovers of self, lovers of money, proud, arrogant, abusive, disobedient to their parents, ungrateful, unholy, inhuman, implacable, slanderers, profligates, fierce, haters of good, treacherous, reckless, swollen with conceit, lovers of pleasure rather than lovers of God, holding the form of religion but denying the power of it" (2 Tim. 3:2-5).

It is much easier to be swept along by the currents of our times where self, money, and pleasure are the priorities of life. Yet, we know that this is in direct opposition to the High Way, God's way. We can never, by our own efforts, overcome the siren call of self, of concupiscence, of the way of the flesh. We should note that St. Paul calls those who walk after their own way "inhuman." Inhuman! That way is broad. It is the path to destruction. Rather, we are called forward to the Way, the Truth and the Life, the narrow way, the strait path. The way that is fully human as God originally created us "in His image and likeness." Fully human is to be fully in the image and likeness of God. In other words, there is no other path of full actualization, absolute happiness, and true meaning outside of relationship with God through the redeeming work of Christ! This path is not a pleasure journey. It will often lead us through the testing in the wilderness.

Walking in the Way will continually challenge and reorder our priorities and worldview. If that isn't occurring, then we need a careful examination of conscience. This is why we each must journey to Gethsemane. We must make this journey over and over. It is here in this garden of choice we will choose my way or God's way. The great question is, will I trust God enough to surrender everything to Him? Will I, like Jesus, trust to the very point of death? Am I convinced; do I with St. Paul "know whom I have believed?" Am I persuaded that "he is able to guard until that Day what has been entrusted to us?" Are we willing, not hypothetically or theoretically, but in actuality, to trust God to the very point of death?

Of course, such trust is not possible until we know who we believe. And even then, we will struggle with maintaining that trust. Adam and Eve knew God, they walked and talked with Him. Yet their trust in Him wavered and failed when the serpent beckoned. Jesus, in Gethsemane cries out "Abba, Father" (Mk. 14:36). Jesus, who is one with the Father, never wavered in His trust that the Father was more than able to raise Him from the dead (see Matt. 20:17-28; Mk. 10:32-45; Lk. 18:31-34). We find our most intimate encounter with God in the Garden of Gethsemane. It is here that St. Paul's words ring clearest, "the Spirit himself intercedes for us with sighs too deep for words: (Rom. 8:26). Just as Jesus in great agony, prayed more earnestly in the Garden, so too in our mortal bodies we cry "Abba! Father!" (Rom. 8:15) as the Spirit "bears witness with our Spirit that we are children of God" (Rom. 8:16).

It is in this personal encounter with God, the loving Father, who has been seeking for us, who ordered the plan of salvation, who through covenants and blessing revealed Himself to a blinded world, that we are called to sonship! As sons and daughters, we are called to put to death the works of the flesh, the results of submitting to the siren call of the triple concupiscence that is our fleshly inheritance. We are called to surrender "my way" so that we might take up our rightful inheritance as the children of God, as joint heirs with Christ and live according to the Spirit, the High Way!

Let's return to the story of the prodigal son in Luke 15. Remember that this parable speaks to us about a young man who, as the younger brother would have a greatly reduced inheritance. He, like many of us, was in a hurry to be able to be his own person with no one putting restrictions upon him. Certainly not the responsibilities of being the father's son. Sacred Scripture tells us that he went to a "far country and there he squandered his property on loose living" (Lk. 15:13).

Think of the younger son; he in effect, says to his father, "you are dead to me." He did not trust his father enough to live as an obedient son. He did not believe that the best for him was available in his father's house. This son then goes to a far country. Adam, and all mankind stained by sin, are in a far country, far from the Father's house. The very House which Jesus tells us has many rooms, or in the old versions, "many mansions."

The allure of exotic locales, the bright lights of the nightlife, all can seem so very enticing. I imagine this young man, in a far country, without the influence of his father, without the order that his father brought to his life. I imagine a modern setting: the first stop the young man makes is to buy a Ferrari! Then a new set of clothes. Off to the club! As he flashed his cash around, buying rounds for everyone, he developed a large group of "friends." A few lines of coke, and he was the life of the party!

You see, in a far land, the land of my way, the father is a distant memory. Scripture calls the son's lifestyle, "loose living." The old Douay-Rheims version calls it "living riotously." It is in this "riotous, loose" living that he succumbs to all three of the triple concupiscence. We often find ourselves in the exact same place! At some point in time, all the resources we can muster fail. Our living is wasted. Emotionally, physically, and especially spiritually, we are bankrupt.

And then famine strikes. The famine that comes from "self-sufficiency". The famine that comes from the empty breadbaskets of the world. The famine that comes from surrender to the inclination toward sin. This is the famine that is the direct result of life lived my way! When we live by "my way" the result is that we perish with hunger.

Lest we think that only those in a "far country" succumb to concupiscence, we cannot overlook the older brother in this parable. He is the one who, by his own admission, has always obeyed the father. He is the one who has always served the father, has never left for a "far country." Yet in his reaction to the celebration of his brother's return, we can discern the effects of concupiscence. Pride of life keeps him from joining the party! After all he has status and position. Lust of the flesh and lust of the eyes figure into the older brother's complaint that there has never been a fatted calf killed for him! Most of us are probably closer to the older brother than the younger brother.

It is so very easy to live in the Father's house and not really, truly be in the "image and likeness" of the Father! It is all too easy to walk "my way" even in the Father's house. This is why we sit through Mass and complain about the length, the music, the homily, the ushers, the noisy kids, etc.! We are acting out the attitudes of the older brother!

We so readily identify with St Paul's lament, "For I do not do the good I want, but the evil I do not want is what I do" (Rom. 7:19). I intend to pray, and yet I start my to-do list in my mind! I intend to listen and participate fully in the Mass, and yet I find myself lost in a world of thoughts that are no different than the "far country." I intend to not covet, but I seem to unceasingly try to "get ahead." I intend to care for and tend to the needs of my fellow man, but the best I can muster are the hollow words, "go in peace, be warmed and filled." Our minds are set on the "things of the flesh." We are in need of regeneration.

So how do we get on the High Way? How do we come to a place where we trust our very lives to God? How do we develop and live the attitude that is expressed of those whose story is told in the 11th chapter of the letter to the Hebrews?

> And what more shall I say? For time would fail me to tell of Gideon, Barak, Samson, Jephthah, of David and Samuel and the prophets—who through faith conquered kingdoms, enforced justice, received promises, stopped the mouths of lions, quenched raging fire, escaped the edge of the sword, won strength out of weakness, became mighty in war, put foreign armies to flight. Women received their dead by resurrection. Some were tortured, refusing to accept release, that they might rise again to a better life (Heb. 11:32-35).

The key to living as "strangers and exiles," as those who "desire a better country," is found in the Garden of Gethsemane. There is no surrender outside of Gethsemane. There is no resurrection without Gethsemane. Gethsemane is the place where the course correction, the move from My Way to High Way occurs. It here, with Jesus as our example, that we lay aside the priorities and passions of this world and accept the eternal will of God as we desire a "better country".

The 12th chapter of the letter to the Hebrews tells us to look "to Jesus the pioneer and perfector of our faith, who for the joy set before him endured the cross, despising the shame, and is seated at the right hand of the throne of God" (Heb. 12:2). Look to Jesus' example. An example of joyful faith in God the Father. The example of enduring even to the shedding of his blood. The example of absolute trust in God, the Almighty to raise him from the dead and restore him to his rightful place! This is our example, and this trust, this High Way is actualized in Gethsemane!

Chapter 15

"Thy Will be Done"

Our Father, who art in heaven, Hallowed be thy name. Thy kingdom come. Thy will be done, On earth as it is in heaven. (Matt. 6:9-10)

During the Sermon on the Mount, Jesus taught the disciples how to pray. He tells them to not pile up a lot of meaningless words like the Gentiles do. Bombasity is of no value. Praying to try and convince others, (or yourself) of your piousness doesn't work. God is not an ATM machine; you can't just use the right PIN number and access all His goodies!

Let's carefully consider the dual request of "Thy kingdom come, Thy will be done on earth as it is in heaven." Oftentimes, we ask for the kingdom of God to come in a future sense. Some point out there in the distant future. Or we ask for His kingdom to reign in some area of our material need. (This is the essence of the "prosperity gospel.) The reality is that God's kingdom exists eternally, all of creation is ultimately subject to Him, to the laws that He has instituted from the forming of the world! Yet He gave man, created a little lower than the angels, free will.

The freedom to choose the Kingdom of Life or the kingdom of death. My way, my will is always the way of death. Only in submission to His will, the High Way is Life. Submission to His will, to His Lordship, to His dominion is the way to life eternal. (And don't slip into the mindset that eternal life only begins after your physical death on earth. You are living your eternal life right now! Some live to earn the "reward" of eternal damnation and punishment. This is truly death. The fires of Hell, apart from God forever, "weeping and gnashing of teeth in outer darkness.") Of course, our inclination towards sin constantly pulls us towards death.

What do we do? We pray; honestly, earnestly, pray "Thy will be done!" Joining Jesus in Gethsemane, we must pray over and over, "not my will." It is notable that the first prayer that Christ taught the disciples is the same prayer He prays in the most difficult moments of His life.

The lesson is clear. Our prayer must be for God's will to be done. St. Augustine clarifies, "May it be so done in me that I shall not resist Thy will" (Augustine of Hippo. 1951. *Commentary on the Lord's Sermon on the Mount with Seventeen Related Sermons*. H. Dressler, Ed., D. J. Kavanagh, Trans. Vol. 11, p. 244. Washington, DC: The Catholic University of America Press.) To pray "Thy will be done" is to pray for God's will to be done in me!

The Our Father corresponds to the prayer in Gethsemane. Consider that Jesus, "the pioneer and perfecter of our faith," prays this knowing that God's will went through the cross. We must understand that to pray for God's will is to lay down our self-life. To pray for God's will is to surrender in complete trust that what God has in store for those who love him is truly indescribable for "eye has not seen, ear has not heard."

We really don't want to face the loss of autonomy. We really do struggle to trust. Yet, this is the call of Christ; "If any man would come after me, let him deny himself and take up his cross daily and follow me. For whoever would save his life will lose it; and whoever loses his life for my sake, he will save it" (Luke 9:23-23). To save our life, to actually have life, we must daily take up our cross, we must deny self, we must lose our life. Sounds backwards, right? Yet this is Jesus' message again and again. He speaks of a grain of wheat that must die to live. He tells us that if we love this world we will die.

Dying to self, dying to the lie of Satan, dying to the world may be the hardest aspect of following Christ. Yet it is perhaps the most important thing we can do to continue in our conversion. It is the path of conversion from the fleshly existence to the life in peace and fidelity with God. This is the call of St. Paul in the first 11 verses of the 6th chapter of his letter to the Romans. St. Paul exhorts us to remember that our baptism into Christ was baptism into His death so that we might "walk in the newness of life." St. Paul tells us that "he who has died is free from sin" (vs 7).

St. Paul continues, "Do not yield your members to sin as instruments of wickedness, but yield yourselves to God as men who have been brought from death to life, and your members to God as instruments of righteousness" (Rom. 6:13). Buried with Christ, now dead to sin, we are to yield, to submit, to obey to God! In the words of an old gospel song; "Trust and obey, for there is no other way, to be happy in Jesus, but to trust and obey."

To truly pray "Thy will be done" requires complete trust in God's intention, His desire, His plan to bring you back from death to life as His child, His adopted son or daughter. Only when we are absolutely convinced that our steps are ordered by God can we fully and completely surrender, not my will but Thine be done. Most of us live as if God is for Sundays and problem days. We often act like God is satisfied with just getting us "saved." Far too often we live our lives as those who are in the world, and only a little bit "not of the world." This is because we give lip service to the repetition of the Our Father, and especially of the prayer, "Thy will be done."

Far too many of us who call ourselves Christians might offer some small part of our lives to God. (Like Sundays and those days that are filled with problems.) But how much do we really mean Thy will be done." How convinced are we that our Father in heaven has our greatest good, our greatest happiness at the very forefront of His will for us?

If we are required to make a choice between God and our finances, our career, what will our choice be? More lip service about how God knows we need money. Or that this is our chosen career path? Or will we submit and surrender to God, our will?

What if we are challenged to choose between God and popularity, acceptance by those around us? Do we act as Peter did on the night he denied even knowing Jesus? Do we compromise our love and commitment to God to not be "embarrassed" or shamed by the Cross of Calvary?

Are we like the rich young ruler that came to Jesus in Luke 18? Do we claim to have kept the commandments and yet wonder how to gain eternal life? Jesus instructed that rich young man to sell all that he had, give it to the poor and then come and follow. Can you hear the gasp? Can you feel the letdown? That young man must have thought, "get rid of all this? This is everything I have!" We know the end of that story, the young man left sad for his possessions were many. How often we are building our own kingdom, our own autonomy. We are still living after the lust of the flesh and eyes, even the pride of life.

Much like Adam and Eve, we distrust anyone other than ourselves, and we certainly do not trust a God who is out there somewhere, or whom we visit with occasionally. God becomes to us a bit like the auntie or uncle that we visit once a year or two. They might even send us a Christmas card or a note on our birthday. We're family, but only just barely. (Can't you almost hear the kids complaining about having to visit that aunt or uncle? Whining about those "old people." Sounds like most Sunday mornings when we get ready to go to Mass, doesn't it?) We complain about how intrusive into our leisure time or preferred activities it is to take time to talk to "the Man upstairs." I mean, if God really cared about us, He would know how important Sundays are for me to: a. get ahead, b. chill out, c. get ready for the week to come! God would certainly appreciate how tired we all are at the end of long day! We can barely get the family to bed at a decent hour, much less spend time before God in prayer. (We aren't so different from the disciples who fell asleep in the Gethsemane as Jesus cried out to the Father.) The choices we make every day; the High Way or my way, Thy will, or my will, is the proof of our sincerity when we ask for the Kingdom of God to come, when we pray for His will to be done on earth, as it is in heaven.

C. S. Lewis says, "There are only two kinds of people in this world, those who say to God, 'Thy will be done', and those to whom God says, in the end, '*Thy* will be done.' Each and every one of us have one and only one absolute choice, one fundamental option: "thy kingdom come" or "my kingdom come." Jesus asks, "Why do you call me 'Lord, Lord,' and not do what I tell you?" (Luke 6:46). We are doing someone's work, we are submitting to someone as lord, we are establishing someone's kingdom. The only question is, our kingdom or God's?

And so, if we really believe what we say, if we really believe that God will raise us up from the dead, then ought we not start living like that now? And how do we live in complete trust? We do so by praying that the Kingdom of God, the Will of God be done in us right here and right now. Jesus made this choice clear when He said, "Not every one who says to me, 'Lord, Lord,' shall enter the kingdom of heaven, but he who does the will of my Father who is in heaven" (Matt. 7:21).

Chapter 16

What is God's Will?

Our difficulty is not that we don't know God's will. Our discomfort comes from the fact that we do know His will, but we do not want to do it. (Henry Blackaby)

What is God's will? As the old saying goes, "if I had a nickel for every time someone asked me that!" After all, if we are called to pray earnestly, fervently, for God's will to be done; if we are to especially pray that His will be done in us; isn't it important for us to know what His will is?

How tragic that so often we view God's will as some big secret that we have to tease out of Him. We act as if this will of God is the great cosmic secret. Some go to great lengths to try to figure out what God's will is. So often, our distrust is such that, like Gideon of old, we put out a fleece to test God's will (See Judges 6). We want a sign from heaven, a loud voice, or any voice! We do tend to overthink this one! God has made His will clear, He is "not willing that any should perish, but that all should come to repentance" (2 Pe. 3:9). As those who have come to repentance, we are reminded of Jesus' dialogue with one of the scribes in the Gospel of St. Matthew. When questioned what the greatest commandment of all is, Jesus replied:

> You shall love the Lord your God with all your heart, and with all your soul, and with all your mind. This is the great and first commandment. And a second is like it, You shall love your neighbor as yourself. (Matt. 22:37-39).

There it is. The will of God! Repent! Turn from your sin-sick self. Come home to the Father! Love Him with all that you are and then love others as you love yourselves. Simple commandments that reveal to us God's will! This is what we are praying for when we pray "Thy will be done on earth as it is in heaven." We are praying that through our rebirth in the waters of baptism, our lives will be formed by our total love for God.

We are committing ourselves to loving God with the totality of our being. It's an undivided love. God is our priority. If we love God with *all* our hearts, souls, minds, and strength, then we won't allow other things to crowd in. We will be singular in our focus on loving God. This is encapsulated in Jesus' words in the Sermon on the Mount, "Seek first his kingdom." Remember that in His kingdom, His will IS done. His commands ARE followed. Not because God is some despot, but because it is in Him that all that is created continues. Yes, God allows us our free will. We can choose our way over His way. We can use our freedom "as a pretext for evil" or we can "live as servants of God" (1 Pe. 2:16). We must be constantly aware that salvation was bought by the nail-pierced hands of Jesus; not by overwhelming force but by love; not by power but by sacrifice. Jesus Christ surrendered His will to the Father so that we might be made alive through His love. David cried out, "O God, you are my God, I seek you, my soul thirsts for you; my flesh faints for you, as in a dry and weary land where no water is" (Ps. 63:1). That my friend is love! "I seek you." You are what I long for! What I thirst for! We too often love the trappings, the blessings, the gifts, rather than the Gift Giver.

Think of the story of Martha and Mary. Martha is busy. She is serving. And she is indignant. (Sounds a bit like the older brother.) Mary simply sits at Jesus' feet. She thirsts for Him, she longs for Him, and so she simply sits at Jesus' feet. And Jesus says that Mary has chosen the better. The better is to love God. To just love Him. I think of Bro. Lawrence who so wanted to experience the presence of God in every detail of daily life. I think of the married couple that can hardly stand to be apart for even a few hours. No, not the immature infatuated couple whose love fades in the difficulties of life, I mean the couple who feels each other's pain, shares each other's joy, finishes each other's thoughts, and completes each other! God does not need us so that He might be complete, but we sure do need Him if we are to be complete!

Too often we think of morally upright actions as the means to happiness. If we act in a certain manner, we will one day be happy. If this was all that was needed, then we would just exhort pagans to act as Christians. This would mean that by acting like a Christian you would become a Christian. We know that the Gospel speaks of faith, grace, and justification. We need to be adopted as the sons and daughters of God through the waters of Baptism. Because through the sacrament of Baptism, we are new creations, there is a new way of acting required. Jesus implores the disciples, "If you love me, you will keep my commandments" (Jhn. 14:15).

Love requires obedience. The subsuming of my will to the One who is worthy of obedience. This was lost on Adam and Eve. They thought they could find happiness and fulfillment through disobedience. Yet, all that they needed for happiness and fulfillment; all that they needed to bring them to their God-given destiny was contained in God's will for them. And the same is true for us. We find ourselves not within ourselves, but within God. We find the abundance of happiness and fulfillment within God, the One who is Love, The One who adopts us as His own and shares all that He is with us through Christ Jesus. It is in obedience that the gate to God's Garden of Abundant Life, Paradise is opened by Christ. It is in obedience to God's commandments that Christ opens that gate for you and me.

When we love God, we want to know Him. To spend time with Him! To be with Him! To share the joy of knowing Him! And when we love Him with the totality of our very being, nothing is of greater importance in our lives than living that love! In fact, the real definition of happiness is communion with God by the gift of the Holy Spirit. This is man's fulfillment. Communion with God is man's happiness. This is where we began:

> "God, infinitely perfect and blessed in himself, in a plan of sheer goodness freely created man to make him share in his own blessed life. For this reason, at every time and in every place, God draws close to man. He calls man to seek him, to know him, to love him with all his strength" (CCC 1).

So that we may share in God's life, that we may share in God's love is why God comes to us! It is why he calls us to seek, know, and love him with all our strength.

This is what St. Paul is referring to in the 5th chapter of his letter to the Ephesians when he speaks of the love of a husband and a wife. St. Paul says that he is speaking of the great mystery of Christ and the Church when he speaks of the sacrificial love of matrimony. A husband who will even sacrifice himself for his wife, a wife who will surrender all that she is for her husband. No thing, no possession, no individual more important than the one spouse to the other. No thing, no possession, no career, no individual greater to the follower of Christ than God! It is here that happiness is found! Happiness on earth, Beatitude in heaven. The common thread to both is charity! Anyone who lives in charity is happy; fulfilled. On earth, charity depends on faith and hope (whence the magisterium of the apostolic Church and the sacraments, which are necessary for sustaining faith and hope). In heaven, beatific charity flows directly from beatific vision: no faith, no hope, no mediation of magisterium and sacraments.

Heaven is pure interpersonal communion with God, perfect participation in the pure interpersonal communion of the Trinity. On earth, we have this interpersonal communion (charity), but it is accompanied by magisterium, sacraments, and charisms. To know God is to know perfect charity, perfect love (see 1 John 4). This perfect love is our call towards God. This was God's command to his chosen people Israel (see Duet. 6). It is His call to His chosen people, the new Israel, the Redeemed.

This is the meaning of "no other gods before me" (Ex. 20:3). The Catechism (CCC 2113) quotes Jesus as it explains, "Man commits idolatry whenever he honors and reveres a creature in place of God, whether this be gods or demons (for example, satanism), power, pleasure, race, ancestors, the state, money, etc. Jesus says, "You cannot serve God and mammon" (Matt 6:24). Many marriages have failed because of misplaced affection. No relationship can be strong, much less thrive in the face of competing affections. Communion is broken in such instances and the same is true for our communion with God. Much of the work of our continuing conversion is the work of placing God on the throne, the pedestal, the center of our very existence. We offer this to God not out of fear or even loathing, but out of gratitude and love.

We hear so much about love. In my experience, love is probably the most common topic in pop music, pop literature, and even homilies. If "all we need is love," we probably better come to a clear understanding of what love really is. So much of our culture's understanding of love focuses on feeling. Love is reduced to a particular feeling that may come and go! That feeling is usually rooted in the thought of "what is in this for me?" Whether it is the "feel good moment" of a physical encounter, or the momentary satisfaction of self through whatever means are at hand.

Often the popular understanding of love is little more than a thinly disguised use of others to satisfy self. Like an infant, we place ourselves in the center of our universe. We expect everything and everyone to somehow further our happiness and fulfillment. We even extend this to God. Our "love" seems dependent on his gratifying our needs and wants. The love that is God, the love that is to be the hallmark of our lives in God is our only legitimate response to God's loving us when we were unlovable.

Much like the prodigal, the father never quit loving his lost child. God has never stopped loving us! The question becomes, "Do I love God with all that I am? Body, mind, and soul?" And if I do, what does that love, that charity look like?

I submit to you that the answer to how we are to love God is modeled by God himself. "For God so loved the world that he gave his only-begotten Son" (John 3:16). God loved you and me in such a way that he gave his one and only Son, the Son of promise to overcome the power of death by his love offered freely on the cross of Calvary! This love, this charity, is sacrificial at its core. Love is first and foremost sacrificial. Not just for the sake of sacrifice, but for the good of the one for whom the sacrifice. This is love. This is God. St. Paul describes this love in action when he writes to the Philippians. He describes Christ as "taking on the form of a servant" (Phil. 2:7). There it is, a servant! This is certainly different than what we commonly consider love to be.

Satan's Great Lie

Satan's greatest deception since the Garden of Eden is the redefining of love. The love we hear about in songs, we see portrayed on TV and in the movies is a love equated with what is good for me. Love is what makes me feel good. Love is what all the world needs, and love is free! Right? Right? Well, no, not exactly. Not even close.

Satan has convinced the world that his view of love, a pathetic substitution, is the real deal. After all, look at what that approach has done for society. The hook-up culture has produced an unimaginable number of single-parent homes, broken hearts, and self-absorbed narcissists. Self-absorption passes for self-love and whatever makes me feel good is what is right, regardless of how that affects you!

I love ice cream. I love my favorite football team (especially when they win!). I love the feeling of warm sunshine on a cold winter day. I love . . ., you fill in the blank! Notice it is all about me! Satan began by telling Adam and Eve that they could be like God. They could control their own actions, their own destiny, their own pleasure, and happiness! It was all about themselves. Ignore what God has said. Don't consider how your actions will impact another. That was the love that Satan offered to Adam and Eve. And it is the same love he pawns off on mankind today.

Today, perhaps more than ever before, this lie is accepted as the social norm. This kind of love is nothing like the love that God is. It is nothing like the love that we are called to have for God and for our neighbor. The truth is that the attitude that is sold as love today is not love at all. Most commonly, it is narcissistic self-indulgence masquerading as love. It is the very thing that caused the rich young man to walk away.

He claimed that he had kept the commandments, and he had loved his neighbor as himself. Jesus told him to "go, sell what you possess and give to the poor, and you will have treasure in heaven; and come, follow me" (Matt 19:21). The young man had "great possessions." He couldn't bear to part with them, even in exchange for eternal life. Do you see the hypocrisy here? Sell your possessions, give to the poor, and heavenly treasure is yours. But he loved his possessions most. He couldn't love his neighbor as himself. He couldn't love with all that he was. No, he loved his possessions above all else. This is the love that is of the world. This is the love that causes a couple to "quit" loving each other because the passage of time has made each one less attractive. Or maybe someone who can offer more fun, more stuff, and more status is available. This is not really love at all.

God's Great Love

The love that is God is a radically different love. The CCC defines this love, charity as "the theological virtue by which we love God above all things for his own sake, and our neighbor as ourselves for the love of God" (CCC 1822). We love God not for the goodies he can provide us with. Not for the "fire insurance" that keeps us from hell. But rather, simply because he is God. He is worthy of our love. He is the source of our love. This charity described in the CCC is a theological virtue. To love God for his own sake is not to love out of fear of punishment, or for the promise of goodies. The Catechism describes the ones who love in this manner as slaves or mercenaries.

Yet, God wants to call us sons and daughters. God wants us to love Him as sons and daughters, in the fullness and freedom of being the children of God. Let's return again to the story of the prodigal son. When he set out to return to his father's house, he intended to go as a servant, a slave. The father sees his son who was lost, now returning home, clothes that wayward young man with the clothes of sonship. He embraces and kisses his son, who was dead, but is now alive. This son is able to freely and fully respond to the one who loved him first, who loved him when he was unlovable, and who loves him as he returns home. So, we too are able to love, because of the One who first loved us. He loved us in the words of St. John, "to the end."

Why did Jesus come and die for us, sinners living in rebellion against God and his ways? Because "God so loved the world that he gave his only-begotten Son" (Jhn 3:16). He gave his Son who came freely, willingly to be "lifted up" as Moses had lifted up a serpent in the wilderness (See Numbers 21:6-9). The children of Israel had complained against God, (again) and were afflicted by the bite of serpents.

Sound familiar? By looking upon the bronze serpent, that God instructed Moses to make and lift up, those stricken by the serpent's fiery bite were saved. Jesus came, obedient to death on the tree of Calvary so that we might partake of the Tree of Life and once again be the children of God, the sons and daughters of the Father Almighty! God, in His great love, redeems us from death and restores us to life in Christ and our only reasonable response is to love Him with all we are.

Living God's Love

Jesus declared that no one has any greater love than to lay down his own life for his friends (see John 15:13). In this same discourse Jesus tells us that we are his friends if we do what he commands us to do. In his final instructions to the disciples before His Passion, Jesus gave a new commandment; "love one another as I have loved you" (John 15:12). If I am filled with the love of God, then the evidence of my life will be love for my neighbor. We, by our love for others, bring the light of God's love to a dark and loveless world. St. John goes so far as to tell us that "He who loves his brother abides in the light, and in it there is no cause for stumbling" (1 Jhn 2:10).

We are to love not in words, after all words are rather cheap. Instead, we are called to love our brother by our actions. By that, it is meant that when we see our neighbor in need, as far as it is possible, we are to provide assistance. We are to minister to not just spiritual needs but to the needs of the hungry, of the weary. St. James tells us that, "Religion that is pure and undefiled before God and the Father is this: to visit orphans and widows in their affliction, and to keep oneself unstained from the world" (James 1:27). It is by our love, our charity for one another that the lost world will see Christ!

The new commandment that Jesus gives the disciples in the Gospel of St. John is that we love one another as he has loved us. Remember we are not talking about the definition of love that Satan has made popular in the world. You know the love that is more about me than about you! No, this is the charity, the love that Jesus demonstrated in his living and dying for us! This love is costly.

The Cost of Charity

The love that we are to have for others has as its source, God. It is God's love that fills us and overflows through us to others. The other starts in the home. St. Paul exhorts husbands to love their wives as Christ loved the Church and gave himself for it (Eph. 5:25). This sacrificial love is what binds families together. This sacrificial love is what Jesus calls us to "abide in." But it is a sacrificial love! It is costly.

In the Sermon on the Mount, Jesus explains how the love of God is to be lived in our lives (Matt. 5:43ff). We are instructed to "love our enemies." We do this so that we may be the sons of our heavenly Father. We do this because even sinners love those who love them. See how this leads back to "while we were yet sinners, (and remember a sinner is by definition one who is at war with God), he died for us." That is the "no greater love" Jesus calls us to have for our neighbors. This is the "perfect" love that casts out fear! This is the love that is possible because God loved us first! We love not only those who can love us back but even those who will persecute and revile us!

We love, not as an animalistic instinct but as an action of the regenerative power of the Holy Spirit forming us into the image and likeness of the last Adam. The Holy Spirit fills us so that we are no longer captive to our own passions, lusts, and fleshly desires. Rather we, filled with the Spirit, are perfected in the image of God by the theological virtue of charity.

This perfecting, or conversion, of forming, is a lifelong process of again and again surrendering my distorted will, my disordered passions, and my misconstrued sense of love to His perfect will. To His perfect love. To His perfect charity expressed in the offering of Jesus the only begotten Son, the Son whom the Father loves to die in my place so that I might "share in His blessed life" forever! This love cost Him everything. It costs me everything that is of this world! It is my free choice to return again and again to the Garden of Gethsemane and willingly surrender myself, my will, my way.

Not because I have to, for that is not love, that is not charity. No, I surrender because I want to, because He first loved me and is filling me with His love. It is no small consequence that it is a lawyer who asks Jesus "Who is my neighbor?" (Lk 10:25-37). You see, it was a legalistic approach to God that sapped all the joy from life and ultimately nailed Jesus to the Cross.

When we freely surrender self to God at Gethsemane, we become truly free, for "if the Son makes you free, you will be free indeed" (John 8:36). True freedom requires sacrificial love, love that holds nothing back. This is the love that defines the Holy Trinity. Love that holds nothing back.

Chapter 17

A Living Sacrifice, Transformed by the Renewal of Your Mind

Watch over yourself, arouse yourself, warn yourself, and regardless of what becomes of others, do not neglect yourself.
(Thomas à Kempis)

We want to go back to the Garden of Eden. We want to live the abundant life that Jesus promised. The life of intimate and full communion with God. Yet, we seem to struggle more than we can handle. It seems that almost every minute of every day presents new challenges and new detours on the path to heaven. Walking with God is no picnic. So, what are we to do?

St. Paul uses the first eleven chapters of his letter to the Romans to lay a doctrinal foundation of sin and salvation, of rebellion and redemption. The 12th chapter turns to the practicalities of life lived in response to salvation, to redemption.

> I appeal to you therefore, brethren, by the mercies of God, to present your bodies as a living sacrifice, holy and acceptable to God, which is your spiritual worship. Do not be conformed to this world but be transformed by the renewal of your mind, that you may prove what is the will of God, what is good and acceptable and perfect" (Rom. 12:1-2).

The only reasonable response to the love and mercy of God is for you and me to be a living sacrifice! This is spiritual worship. This is costly worship. This is costly love, charity. St. Paul asks us to offer our bodies and our minds! Sounds like Jesus' declaration of the greatest commandment, to love God with the entirety of our being!

Jesus made clear that those who save their lives will lose their lives, but "he who loses his life for my sake will save it" (Lk. 9:24). How can this be? The Passion of Christ is always accompanied by the Resurrection! It is the resurrected Christ that lives in us by his Resurrection. Yet, how can He live fully in us unless we fully surrender our self-life. How can we truly worship if we hold to our worldly self. How can we expect any form of happiness or fulfillment if the opening words of Romans apply to us?

> So they are without excuse; for although they knew God they did not honor him as God or give thanks to him, but they became futile in their thinking and their senseless minds were darkened. Claiming to be wise, they became fools, and exchanged the glory of the immortal God for images resembling mortal man or birds or animals or reptiles. Therefore God gave them up in the lusts of their hearts to impurity, to the dishonoring of their bodies among themselves, because they exchanged the truth about God for a lie and worshiped and served the creature rather than the Creator, who is blessed for ever! Amen" (Rom. 1:21-25).

What a juxtaposition of belief and practice! When Adam and Eve chose their will over God's command and disobeyed, they became the parents of all who would "exchange the truth about God for a lie." They became the parents of those who worship the creature, self.

Those who live after the rebellious way of Adam and Eve's sin have "become fools." Their minds are fixed on worldly things. They only see what feels good, what tastes good, what satisfies in this moment. They are what St. Paul rightly describes as "slaves to sin" (Rom. 6:6). This is all about answering the question; "which master do you serve?" We like to think that we serve no one, we are our own master. But the person who serves only self is subject to "the law of sin and death" (Rom. 8:2). This is the condition of all who have rejected Christ.

Sometimes our rejection of Christ is not really overt, but it is rejection, nonetheless. When we live for ourselves first, when we act for ourselves first, we are serving the law of sin and death. We are living as those in rebellion against God. We are declaring that not Your will, but mine is our way of life. (Well, actually death!) Just being religious is not enough. Still being conformed to the values, priorities, and ways of the world is to live as one who worships the creature, not the Creator.

St. Paul speaks at length about this very issue in many of his writings. (See Rom. 6, 1 Cor. 6, Gal. 5, Eph. 5, Col. 3.) Our conforming to the heavenly world, to the will of God is accomplished not by trading one set of moral dos and don'ts lists for another.

We aren't transformed just by trading immoral behavior for moral behavior. Our own efforts are never enough. Conforming to God is accomplished by transformation. Transformation is the work of the Holy Spirit in us. It is the Spirit that gives us life (See 2 Cor. 3:6). It is this life that is the life of the New Covenant in Christ. The life of one who is being transformed. A life where by God's grace, sin has no dominion over us! Can you imagine garments of purest white? The pure radiance of God's presence lighting our faces much like Moses as he came down from meeting with God on Mt. Sinai? (Ex. 24:29-35) This is transformation! This is a new creation.

Thanks be to God for his Son, the last Adam who makes all things new. In whom we are made a new creation. In whom we are renewed in mind and soul! It is this renewal, this sacrificial conforming to the image and likeness of Jesus, and this transforming of our mind to the mind that sees as God sees that St. Paul is speaking to. Those who have received the saving grace of God reject the works of the flesh and of a futile mind and are rather "transformed by the renewal of your mind."

The body as a living sacrifice is detailed throughout St. Paul's writings as we are exhorted to not submit to the passions of the flesh. St. Paul tells us to "put to death the deeds of the body" (Rom. 8:13), the deeds that lead to death. These deeds are deeds based on self-love. The charity we are being filled with by the Holy Spirit leads us to act in a different manner, to use our bodies for the glory of God, rather than the satisfaction of self. (Perhaps here is a bit of an insight into the martyrs as their bodies were battered, broken, mutilated, and destroyed in the most horrific manner, and yet so many of the martyrs died with the praises of God on their lips!)

Rather we are called to live as the citizens of a heavenly Kingdom. Those who act prudently, temperately, chastely, and with charity.

It is not enough to merely imitate certain actions. Even the Pharisees acted with a high degree of self-righteousness. We must be transformed. We must be made into a new creation in the last Adam. We must develop the heart and the mind that are of the sons and daughters of God. We must have a heart of stone replaced with a heart of flesh. We must have a mind that is fixed on the "things that are above, not on things that are on earth" (Col. 3:2).

This only happens by the renewing of our mind. We are to have "the mind of Christ" (1 Cor. 2:16). Our worldview, the way we think about activities, possessions, and people must flow from the Holy Spirit in us. The eyes of our understanding must be opened to see as God sees, through the eyes of the Gospel if you will. To see the unlovable as deserving of love. To see the unforgivable as deserving of forgiveness. To see the riches of this world as something that will rust and decay. To apprehend the Kingdom, the one that eye has not seen nor ear hath heard about. To be among those who by living as a sacrifice in worship to God, transformed and renewed; living as "strangers and exiles, living as those who are "seeking a homeland;" to be among those is to be among those whom

"God is not ashamed to be called their God!" (See Heb 11:14-17.) This transformation is a lifelong conversion, an ongoing formation. St. Paul speaks at length about this process, about this journey in the 4th chapter of his letter to the Ephesians. He speaks of attaining the "measure of the stature of the fulness of Christ," of growing "up in every way into him who is the head, into Christ."

Chapter 18

Transformation, The Journey of a Lifetime

The self-denial which is pleasing to Christ consists in little things. This is plain, for opportunity for great self-denials does not come every day. Thus, to take up the cross of Christ is no great action done once for all, it consists in the continual practice of small duties which are distasteful to us.

(John Henry Newman

As we contemplate the way of transformation, of renewal, we understand that this is a process. It is a "line upon line, precept upon precept" approach to living. It is literally a metamorphosis of our being. When we think of examples of metamorphosis, we think of the caterpillar that goes into a cocoon and emerges. Metamorphosized as a beautiful butterfly. Our old, ugly, sinful approach to life is transformed, and metamorphosed into something beautiful! The Greek term, *metemorphothe* is used only once in the Gospels. There it is used to describe Jesus on the Mount of Transfiguration (the mountain of "transformation" - same word, *metemorphothe*): "And he was transfigured before them, and his face shone like the sun, and his garments became white as light" (Matt. 17:2). We are called to this kind of *metemorphothe,* this kind of transformation.

While that transformation won't be complete until the day of Christ's return and "until everything is subject to him until there be realized new heavens and a new earth in which justice dwells" (CCC 671), we understand that even in the minutiae of our daily living we are either conforming to the world or being transformed for the world to come. Much like the prodigal son, our Heavenly Father calls for the finest robes, robes of pure white, robes of righteousness to be placed on our shoulders. In heaven, we will be clothed in white, pure, and complete in Jesus. This is promised to those who refrain from the sins of the flesh, from spiritual death and rather live a life of holiness in Christ.

St. Paul begs us to "walk in a manner worthy of the calling to which you have been called" (Eph. 4:1). He then describes what that transformed walk looks like: "with all lowliness and meekness, with patience, forbearing one another in love, eager to maintain the unity of the Spirit in the bond of peace" (Eph. 4:2,3). Notice again the focus, not on self, but on others.

The metamorphosis of becoming a new creation in Christ is a radical reorienting of the mind to obedience to God. It's not just adopting a new set of rules, replacing the old works of the flesh with a new set of laws. St. Paul replaces the works of the flesh, not with works of the law, but rather with the fruit of the Spirit! (Gal. 5:19-22). The mind of one who submits his will to God in Gethsemane is no longer a center of depravity (Rom. 1: 18-32), rather "we have the mind of Christ" (1 Cor. 2:16) who always perfectly did the Father's will.

Our obedience to the will of the Father is modeled on Christ. From His prayer in the Garden of Gethsemane to every action of his life, and especially his death, Christ lived the Father's will perfectly. He lived and died as an offering of charity, of perfect love. The perfect love of the Father towards you and me. And now we are called to walk in this way. Patiently, peacefully, even meekly! For the mind of Christ is always to do the will of his Father. The mind of Christ is not self-seeking, not self-serving. All that Christ did was from charity, all that we do, when we are being transformed is from charity.

A renewed mind is the mind of the last Adam. The first Adam surrendered his mind to the will of self. The last Adam surrenders his mind to the will of the Father. That is the renewed mind, the mind that is surrendered to the Father. Would you be renewed by the transformation of your mind? Then be "obedient from the heart." Be a "slave of God" (Rom. 6:22) and be free from sin and death. For after all, St. Paul says, "the return you get is sanctification and its end, eternal life" (Rom. 6:22). And after all, we do want eternal life in the Garden of Paradise! A renewed mind is a renewed understanding of reality, a reordering of priorities, and a renewed course of action. How do we progress on this journey of transformation? This journey of renewal?

Chapter 19

How to Renew Your Mind

We shall never be able to know ourselves, except we endeavor to know God. By considering His greatness, we discover our own baseness; by contemplating His purity, we discover our own filthiness, and beholding His humility, we shall discover how far we are from being truly humble. (TERESA OF AVILA)

I wish we had a formula, three easy steps to the renewal of your mind. Three easy steps that would transform you into the citizen of Heaven you are meant to be. It's just not that easy. Like gardening, transformation is hard work. Just ask anyone who has ever tried to transform their body. Dieting is never easy. Exercise is exhausting and can be painful. But if you are going to transform your body, if you are going to get in shape, hard work is necessary. The price must be paid. Weeding the garden, fertilizing the plants, watering when the summer is at its hottest, it's all hard work. But that effort is required to bring in a harvest.

A couple of years ago we planted about 60 okra plants. (It's a Southern thing, y'all!) After nursing the little tender plants, making sure that the weeds didn't overwhelm the tender shoots, watering diligently, we had a harvest! We had to harvest the okra every day! We could not miss even a single day, or the okra would grow too large to be good for eating. We harvested over 100 pounds of okra that year. We fed the neighborhood with okra. We ate okra, we canned okra, and we even froze okra. We are still enjoying the fruits of our labor from that okra harvest. This is the same way the renewing of our mind, and the transformation of our lives takes place. Assuming we are taking care of the basics, reading Sacred Scripture, praying, and following the precepts of the Church, there is still more to be done.

Our entire existence has trained our minds to prioritize the things of the world. The temporal things that seem so important on this earth. Power, possessions, position, performance! These are all the outworking of the mind subjected to the triple concupiscence. This is the mind that treasures this world! This is the mind that is enslaved to sin. This is the mind that really doesn't believe God, doesn't really trust him., this is the same mind that the prodigal son possessed.

You see when our mind is unrenewed we are conformed to the world. How do we turn from the pursuit of power, possessions, position, and performance? By the renewal of our minds. This is the key to metemorphothe, transformation. This is the key to living as the adopted sons and daughters of God. This is recreating our worldview; how we see and act toward all that occurs to us, and in us. This worldview is the bent of our life. Unrenewed is bent towards sin, and renewed is bent towards the things of the heavenly realm.

> *You must no longer walk as the Gentiles walk, in the futility of their minds; they are darkened in their understanding, alienated from the life of God because of the ignorance that is in them, due to their hardness of heart; they have become callous and have given themselves up to licentiousness, greedy to practice every kind of uncleanness. (Eph.4: 17-19)*

The Hard Heart

The path of renewal begins in the heart. I know we are talking about the renewal of the mind, but did you just read what St. Paul said, alienated from the life of God because of . . . ignorance . . . due to the hardness of their heart?" Sin has hardened our hearts. Sin has left us ignorant of God. How is our heart softened? How is it made receptive to God? First, our heart must be broken. We must confront the evil of our sin and be broken before God for our sin. For our disobedience. For our rebellion. With St. Peter, we must declare, "I am a sinful man!" We must truly repent! Completely and willfully reject this world and all its disordered acts; all of its disobedience to God. It is the hardness of our hearts that will not submit to the Lordship of Jesus Christ. It is the hardness of our hearts that blinds our minds to the supremacy of Christ over all.

The prophet Ezekiel looked forward to a day when the hearts of stone that had filled God's people would be replaced by a heart of flesh. "A new heart I will give you, and a new spirit I will put within you; and I will take out of your flesh the heart of stone and give you a heart of flesh" (Ezek. 36:26). This is the new creation of the new covenant which is Christ Jesus.

Those that are renewed with a heart of flesh are called God's people. (Jer. 31:33 ff). We must realize that this is the work of the Holy Spirit. In only one other place in the Greek New Testament does the word *renewal* appear; Titus 3:5 says, "he saved us, not because of deeds done by us in righteousness, but in virtue of his own mercy, by the washing of regeneration and renewal in the Holy Spirit." This renewal is not by our efforts but by the renewing and regenerative work of the Holy Spirit within us. It is this work of the Holy Spirit that causes St. Paul to declare in 1 Cor. 6:19, "Do you not know that your body is a temple of the Holy Spirit within you, which you have from God?" We are being transformed from the hardhearted ignorance of God into the very image of God according to St. Paul. "And we all, with unveiled face, beholding the glory of the Lord, are being changed (*metemorphothe,* transformed) into his likeness from one degree of glory to another; for this comes from the Lord who is the Spirit" (2. Cor. 3:18-19). Transformed into his likeness! How are we transformed? How is our heart turned from hardness, from stone to that which is soft and pliable and open to God? By beholding the glory of the Lord, by continually gazing upon Christ and the mysteries of His glories! (Kind of sounds like Adoration and the Rosary!!!)

The Ignorant Mind

The unrenewed mind is a mind that is ignorant. Ignorant of the things and ways of God. It is a mind that cannot comprehend the glory and mercy of God. Did you catch that? "because of the ignorance that is in them." Eyes that are blind to see as God sees. Priorities that are established in ignorance of the Way of God.

The next step in transformation, in the renewal of our minds, is the knowledge of God. According to St. Jerome, "Ignorance of Scripture is ignorance of Christ." St. Paul reminds us "So faith comes from what is heard, and what is heard comes by the preaching of Christ" (Rom. 10:17). We must have our minds filled with the word of God if we are to have the "mind of Christ." Remember when as a kid you heard the old adage, "You are what you eat?" Well, in the things of the mind, our worldview, we are what we put into our minds.

We can fill our hearts, our minds with the constant barrage of trash that the culture all around us shovels at us, or we can be filled with the things of God and by so doing, be renewed. An hour of mindless TV or an hour reading God's Word? The choice is simple, the results are out of this world! The knowledge we fill ourselves with is either transformative or conformative. One is the path of God's children; the other is the path of death and destruction.

Be renewed by what you feed your mind. Overcome the ignorance of God that is the result of sin. Overcome ignorance by the power of the Holy Spirit working in you as you fill your mind with God! And we fill our minds with God as we learn of, contemplate, and explore the mysteries of Christ. Of Emmanuel, God with us. For it is the preaching of Christ, not the lessons of prosperity and wellness that transforms us. It is not some pop psychology presentation masquerading as a sermon or homily that brings the heart-softening, mind-renewing work of the Holy Spirit to bear in our lives. No, it is the preaching of Christ and Him crucified.

God so loved us, that instead of leaving us in the unrenewed place with death as our only future, He sent His Son, Christ to be offered up and crucified so that we might be transformed from the lost to the living. From reprobate to regenerated. From those banished from the Garden to those invited to the Garden of Paradise to eat at the Father's table! You are only free from the constricting conforming to this world if you are free in the Son, for whom the Son has set free is free indeed!

Chapter 20

Practical Steps Towards Renewal

As often as this life's idle show tries to charm you; as often as you see in the world some empty display—transport yourself in mind to Paradise, aim to be now what you will be hereafter.
St. Jerome)

So how then should we act? Let me suggest the idea of RESET. We need to reset our thinking, reset our vision, and reset our words. Remember that you can go through the effort of doing these things externally, but it takes the Holy Spirit replacing a heart of stone, it takes the Holy Spirit's work on us from the inside out to bring true and complete renewal and transformation. We must cooperate with Him. He will not force this upon us. This is the movement from seeing Christ as only our Savior to surrendering to Him as our Lord. It is not an easy journey. Nicodemus the Hagiorite wrote way back in the late 1700's:

> once the eyes become accustomed to looking passionately upon the mature beauty of living bodies; once the eardrums are accustomed to the pleasing sounds of certain songs; once the sense of smell is delighted by the fragrances of myrrh and aromatic things; once the tongue and the mouth taste or rather become accustomed to the rich and tasty foods; and finally, once the sense of touch is accustomed to fine and soft clothing—who will be able after that, even if one is most eloquent and persuasive, to convince people that what they have up to now enjoyed is not a true and rational pleasure, but on the contrary an irrational and temporal one?[12]

Sounds like it could have been written yesterday! It is the same battle we fight today and every day of our continuing conversion. How do we truly move from conformity to this world, to transformation for the world that is to come? You must be made new. You must completely reset. Let's look at how to RESET.

---

[12] Nicodemos of the Holy Mountain, _Nicodemos of the Holy Mountain: A Handbook of Spiritual Counsel_, ed. John Farina, trans. Peter A. Chamberas, The Classics of Western Spirituality (New York; Mahwah, NJ: Paulist Press, 1989), 77.

Reset Your Mind

Have you ever noticed how easily your mind is turned to the wrong things?? Impure thoughts, jealous thoughts, thoughts that violate the dignity of another? Thoughts of hopelessness, of defeat and despair? Thoughts of anger and abandonment? These are the thoughts of the unrenewed mind. These are the patterns of the mind blinded by Satan. To overcome this thought pattern, we ought to heed the words of St. Paul in Philippians 4:8, "Finally, brethren, whatever is true, whatever is honorable, whatever is just, whatever is pure, whatever is lovely, whatever is gracious, if there is any excellence, if there is anything worthy of praise, think about these things." Each of these exhortations is a direct refuting of the unrenewed mind. Each of these is directed towards the glory of Christ in us, in others, and in Christ himself. Our surest course correction is to banish the "stinking thinking" of an unrenewed mind by immediately resetting our thoughts.

Memorize a passage of Sacred Scripture and call it to mind at the first sign of thoughts that are opposed to the transformation that God is bringing about within you. This is not a magic talisman or incantation! It is a recentering of ourselves in the love and mercy of our Heavenly Father. It is a renewal of our faith in His victory in our lives and in our hearts brought by the sacrifice He made for you and me.

The prophet Isaiah tells us, "You keep him in perfect peace, whose mind is stayed on you, because he trusts in you." A mind that is stayed, or fixed on God is a mind in perfect peace. Reset your mind on God through his word so that you might be transformed, at peace as his child! It is notable that St. Paul's words to the Philippians also speak to the peace of God.

When we are transformed by the Spirit, we are no longer at war with God and His peace fills every area of our lives! (Here's a bonus idea! Do you find your mind drifting during Mass or prayer? Reset by immediately calling to mind a passage of Scripture. This will help you fully concentrate on God and what he is about at that moment!)

The Book of Psalms opens with a message of blessing to the transformed man. This is the man who meditates on the instruction of the Lord 24/7. This man is the man who is "like a tree planted by streams of water, that yields its fruit in its season, and its leaf does not wither. In all that he does, he prospers" (Ps. 1:3). He yields his fruit in due season. What is the fruit? What is his prospering? I would submit that it is nothing short of the "fruits of righteousness" (Phil. 1:11) the fruits of the Spirit. Sounds like life in the Garden, the life of communion with God. These are the things that are eternal. These are the thoughts that lead in the way everlasting. Reset your thoughts, reset your mind!

Reset Your Vision *"Turn my eyes away from seeing vain things"* (Ps. 118:37 LXX)

Ever notice that what you see can lead you to an unrenewed mind? To disaster? Satan knew this when he first approached Eve in the Garden of Eden. He promised that Eve's eyes would be opened. She would see as God sees! What an out-and-out lie! Her eyes were blinded to the things of God and so the problem of vision has plagued mankind ever since. Satan always promises enlightenment, entertainment, pleasure, and insights. He does this by bombarding us with visual stimulation that captivates our hearts. That leads to conformity with the world. Eve failed to guard her vision, her eyes.

Our eyes can lead us to sin! (Jesus said it clearly in Matthew 5:29.) Our "eye is the lamp of the body. So, if your eye is sound, your whole body will be full of light; but if your eye is not sound, your whole body will be full of darkness" (Matt. 6:22). That which we gaze upon will enter into our heart, good or evil. That which enters our heart will control our mind. Our eyes can lead us to covet. Our eyes can lead us to doubt. This is what happened in the Garden of Eden. Satan tells her eyes would be opened! She would see! She would see as God sees!

Remember, God walked and talked with Adam and Eve in the cool of the day. They had a direct, firsthand, personal relationship with God. Eve is promised the same vision as God! She would know good from evil. She would see it all! Evil was and still is a "delight to the eyes" (Gen. 3: 6). The story goes on, "Then the eyes of both (Adam and Eve) were opened." The lamp of the body was opened to evil.

Darkness filled their whole body. They no longer loved God with their whole being. They couldn't. Their whole body was full of the darkness that their eyes had beheld and received. They no longer loved their neighbor, (each other) as they loved themselves. No, they saw that they were naked. Now nakedness was a door to evil. A door to selfishness. And so, they were ashamed. Ashamed of the evil that filled their eyes and now filled their hearts.

Doesn't this describe the affliction that so often troubles our souls? We need to reset our vision. We need to reset what our eyes behold. It is not enough to just have a list of what not to look at. We need a redirection. An old gospel song says,

"Turn your eyes upon Jesus, Look full in His wonderful face, and the things of earth will grow strangely dim, in the light of His glory and grace." There my friends, is the reset of vision that we most desperately need. To see Jesus. To see His love, His grace and mercy! To see Him, the Lamb slain from the foundation of the world. The one who loved us to the end.

The letter to the Hebrews instructs us to "look to Jesus." He is the "Author and Perfecter" of our faith. When we gaze upon Jesus, when we sit with Mary at His feet, listening and beholding, our lives are changed! We cannot look at Him and the filth of this world in the same look. We need to reset our vision to see Jesus. Hear the words of St. Paul, "For it is the God . . . who has shone in our hearts to give the light of the knowledge of the glory of God in the face of Christ" (2 Cor. 4:6). St. Paul is speaking about those who have been blinded by the god of this world. Those who live in darkness cannot see. Those who only look to the cares of today. But thanks be to God, He has shone the light of His love upon all who will believe and receive the grace and mercy of God the Father through Jesus the Son, by the power of the Holy Spirit.

When we reset our eyes to see Jesus, we see the glory of God! The glory of God in Christ's face. I know you are thinking where can I see the face of Christ? Let me suggest two specific ways.

First, the regular practice of Adoration. Praying and meditating on Christ, in the presence of the Blessed Sacrament. Most local Catholic parishes have chapels of perpetual adoration. Nothing resets our vision quite like Adoration. Especially if we pray the Rosary and meditate on the mysteries of Christ's life! You will see Jesus!

Second, follow the example of St. Teresa of Calcutta, (Mother Teresa), she said, "I see Jesus in every human being. I say to myself, this is hungry Jesus, I must feed him. This is sick Jesus . . . I must wash him and tend to him." We can see Jesus in every person. Yes, even the slow driver on the freeway! The noisy kid distracting in Mass, the interfering in-law, the beggar on the street corner! When we "see Jesus" in each person, we will act in the will of God, loving our neighbor, "Jesus' as ourselves.

What a different world! What a different worldview! Look to Jesus, see Jesus, turn your eyes to Jesus, and this world will grow dim!

Reset Your Words "For out of the abundance of the heart the mouth speaks. The good man out of his good treasure brings forth good, and the evil man out of his evil treasure brings forth evil" (Matt. 12:34-35)

Ever said something and instantly regretted it? Ever been challenged by someone over some passing remark you made, even as just a little joke? Our words have power. If our eyes let good or evil into our hearts, our words provide evidence of what is actually in our hearts. We can stop and reset our words BEFORE we speak so that even our words reflect our love for God and neighbor. St. James calls the tongue "a fire . . . a restless evil, full of deadly poison" (Jas 3:8). Wow! What we say comes from what we fill our hearts with. If we fill our hearts with fire, with hate, with evil, then our words will lead us away from God's will and God's way. Jesus makes it even more clear in the Gospels of St. Luke and St. Matthew when he says that out of the abundance of our heart; the abundance, good or evil; this is what drives and forms our speech.

We reset our speech when our heart is remade by the Holy Spirit. We reset our speech by filling our minds with the Word of God. We reset our speech by what we hear. We reset our speech by managing what we see. We are renewed, we are transformed as evidenced by the words we say.

Years ago, there was a TV show that was very popular. The host, Art Linkletter, interviewed children. These kids just said whatever came to mind. Art opined that the best people to interview were kids or people over 70. His reasoning was that kids didn't know any better than to say whatever they were thinking, and old folks didn't care what people thought about what they were saying. In either case, the answers came straight from the heart. Some innocent and some not quite so much. While we might find some of the unfiltered answers amusing, we wouldn't necessarily find those answers to be wise, or reflective of the ways of God.

This is what St. Paul is referring to when he tells the Ephesians, "Let no evil talk come out of your mouths, but only such as is good for edifying, as fits the occasion, that it may impart grace to those who hear" (Eph. 4:29). Only good, uplifting words. Words that lead to the grace of God! Try that the next time someone cuts you off as you drive out of the church parking lot after Mass! Our call is to love our neighbor as ourselves. Our words speak (pun intended) to and are an instrument of the transformation of our minds! "Oh, be careful let mouth what you say, for your Father up above, looks down in tender love, so be careful little mouth what you say."

Chapter 21

The Garden of Resurrection,
He Calls You by Name

And He walks with me, And He talks with me,
And He tells me I am His own!
(C. Austin Miles)

A few chapters ago we spoke of how God was the constant Gardener, the one who has always been seeking us. Ever calling us to Himself. We recall how God called for Adam and Eve as He walked through the Garden of Eden in the cool of the day. The Garden of Eden was the Garden of Life, it was there that God breathed the very breath of life into mankind. It was the Garden of Communion with God. Yet, by Adam and Eve's sin, the Garden of Eden became the Garden of Death, of Separation, and Desolation.

The only way to communion with God again, the only way back to life in Him is through the Garden of Gethsemane. It is in the Garden of Gethsemane that the Passion of Christ, the offering of the life of one for all; the offering of the Lamb of God slain from the foundation of the world begins in earnest. It is no small coincidence that the tomb of Jesus is located in a garden (see John 19:41). The path to life always goes through Gethsemane.

We must lay down our life and be made alive in Christ, for as St. Paul says, "I have been crucified with Christ; it is no longer I who live, but Christ who lives in me" (Gal. 2:20). And only then do we arrive at the Garden of Resurrection. The garden of Life and that in Christ. Jesus has taught us to offer up our very being as sacrifice to God. Our will and our way, fully and completely surrendered to Him.

In this place of sacrifice, this place where we lay our lives down so that we might take up the life that is ours in Christ, we are hungry for, eager to, and needing to meet God Himself. Jesus has taught us to offer up our very being as sacrifice to God. Our will and our way fully and completely surrendered to Him. In this place of sacrifice, this place where we lay our lives down so that we might take up the life that is ours in Christ, we are hungry for, eager to, and needing to meet God Himself.

We need the assurance that our sacrifice is not foolish. We need the assurance that God did not simply die on the Cross. St. Paul says, "If for this life only we have hoped in Christ, we are of all men most to be pitied" (1 Cor. 15:19). If only in this life! If only here and now, why make the sacrifice? If only here and now, why be singled out as different, as misguided, as delusional? What kind of god asks for the sacrifice of our lives if this is all there is? We have been in the Garden of Eden and experienced the abundance of life in the graces of God's original plan. We have been with Christ in the Garden of Gethsemane where His Passion is real, His offering of His life made present.

We know He died and was buried in a tomb. After all, that's the story of every religious zealot throughout history, they all die and are buried. Jesus is not just another religious zealot. No, He is the Lamb slain to redeem the lost. To restore creation. To bring us home to Heaven. He is the last Adam, the obedient Son. The One who brings life, and that more abundantly to all who will obey His command. But St. Paul declares that "in fact Christ has been raised from the dead, the first fruits of those who have fallen asleep. For as by a man came death, by a man has come also the resurrection of the dead" (1 Cor. 15:20-21). There is a resurrection! Our bodies will rise again. When we see Jesus, we shall be like Him! This is the word of the Lord. It is the promise of God.

And so, we come to the Garden of Resurrection. Let's set the scene: It's early in the morning, so early it's still dark. Mary Magdalene and other women have come to the tomb to tend to the body of Jesus. When they arrive, they find an empty tomb. Jesus is not there. St. John's Gospel relates how Mary Magdalene told Peter and John that Jesus' body had been taken.

They did not yet know that He must rise from the dead. Mary Magdelene stood at the tomb, brokenhearted. Jesus, the One who had shown her compassion. Jesus, the One who freed her from the demons that possessed her. Jesus, the One who had spoken of life and that more abundantly, was Himself dead and now His body was missing. Stolen. Carried away. She could not even offer Him dignity in burial. Sorrow and sadness overwhelm her.

Through her tears, she encounters two angels and as she turns from those angels, she encounters the "gardener" (John 20:11 ff). The Gardener, the Master Gardener, the Master Gardener who planted a Garden in Eden, the Master Gardener who agonized in the Garden of Gethsemane, simply asks "Woman, why are you weeping? Whom do you seek?" Oh, the piercing question from God Himself. How it changes everything! Why are you consumed with the sorrows of this sin-sick world? Why does the pain of bodily death devastate you so? Is the parting so final that you have no more hope? The questions of Jesus are loaded with such probing into the human condition. The condition of our lives. And then He asks the question of all questions: "Whom do you seek?"

It is the question we must answer over and over again. It is the question that leads us to Gethsemane where we either willingly and completely submit to the lordship of God Almighty, or we join Adam and Eve in rebellion and live as we choose, in answer to the siren song of Satan. "Whom do you seek?" How will you answer? Your answer changes everything. Are you still living with the prodigal, with only the leftovers that the pigs wouldn't eat? Still running from the Father? Still hiding with Adam and Eve after the Fall? Or does your answer place you in the presence of the Father, where He calls for the robes of a son or daughter, the ring of family?

Mary didn't recognize Jesus. Her eyes were blinded with grief. With the loss of hope. Her eyes were blinded by the cares and sorrows of broken dreams. In this moment, the garden was no longer a place of abundance, of fellowship. Rather, her Jesus was dead, and his Body was missing. She cannot see that the Master Gardener is Jesus Himself!

And then the most powerful, most moving word she could hear flowed from the lips of the Gardener, "Mary." Hear it again, "Mary." Jesus called her by name. The One by whom all things were made, the One who is the Word which brought all that is into being, that One called her by name!

Just as God walked through the Garden of Eden on that fateful day so very long ago calling for Adam and Eve, now He calls Mary by name. He calls all who will seek Him, all whom He calls, He calls by name. The prophet Isaiah declares to the Children of Israel, and it applies to you and I, the new Children of Israel in Christ, "Fear not, for I have redeemed you; I have called you by name, you are mine" (Isa. 43:1). He has called each one of us by name! (see CCC 2167). God knows you by name, God calls you by name!

When He called for Adam and Eve, it was to be in communion with them. To share His blessed life. To walk with them. To talk with them. And now it is you and I He calls to that life of communion. It is you and I that He calls by name to share in His blessed life.

Not only does He call us by name, but God tells us that we are His! We belong to Him. We have truly become His prized possession. St. John clearly tells us, "You belong to God" (1 John 4:4 NABRE). Outside of Christ, you belonged to the world. Or in other words, you belonged to death.

You, like Adam and Eve, were banished from the Garden of God. Outside of Christ, we had no claim, no right of entry, no standing before God. We had passed from life into death. We belonged to the world and its ruler! God had a better plan:

> But now in Christ Jesus you who once were far off have been brought near in the blood of Christ . . . So then you are no longer strangers and sojourners, but you are fellow citizens with the saints and members of the household of God, built upon the foundation of the apostles and prophets, Christ Jesus himself being the cornerstone, in whom the whole structure is joined together and grows into a holy temple in the Lord; in whom you also are built into it for a dwelling place of God in the Spirit. (Eph. 2:13, 19-22)

That's what it means to be God's possession, to belong to Him. That's what it means when He calls us, you, and me by name. We are "fellow citizens with the saints." We are "members of the household of God." The very "dwelling place of God in the Spirit." No longer far off but now made His sons and daughters. He calls us His children, and He calls us by name.

God knows you personally. He knows your temptations. He knows your hurts and pains. He knows your brokenness. He offers His healing, His comfort, and His wholeness to you and to me. He loves us so much that we are God's children now; "it does not yet appear what we shall be, but we know that when he appears we shall be like him, for we shall see him as he is" (1 John 3:2).

Mary's response is instructive. Listen to her words when she realizes it is the Risen Savior, Jesus Himself who has conquered death, hell, and the grave. Listen to her response when she realizes that the Lover of our souls calls her by name: "Rab-boni!" "Teacher!" "Master and Lord!"

She even went to the disciples and told them "I have seen the Lord!" She had seen Jesus. Her eyes had been opened, and she heard Him call her by name.

How about you? He is calling you by name. He is asking you to receive Him as Teacher, Master, and Lord. Many years ago, the theme song of a popular TV show reminded us that "sometimes you want to go where everybody knows your name." (Gary Portnoy, "Where Everybody Knows Your Name"). Our names are important. They identify us as unique individuals of incredible worth. Oftentimes, our very identity is wrapped up in our name. Our friends and our family call us by our names. God, our Father calls you and I by name, how can we do anything but respond as Mary did? Rab-boni, Teacher, Master, Lord, and Friend! Here in the Garden of Resurrection, the Garden where death has been defeated and Life has won, in this Garden, we are transported to that place in the gardens of God where, like Adam like Eve, our Father calls us by name! The secret of life is to live in this place. Walk with Him. Talk with Him. Commune with Him. Share in His blessed life.

Chapter 22

The Garden of Heaven (Eternal Paradise)

That angel who had received the sword which excluded from Paradise, beheld the key which was to open it in the Cross, and no longer opposed himself to the entrance.
(St. PETER DAMIAN)

When we think of heaven, we usually picture a place where cute little angels sit on clouds playing harps. We see God as an old father time figure who benevolently shares those clouds with our family and pets that have died. I mean, after all, don't all dogs go to heaven? The reality of heaven couldn't be further from that picture. (It is worth noting that any description of the Garden of Heaven will be woefully inadequate. St. Paul says, "eye has not seen, nor ear heard, nor the heart of man conceived of what God has prepared for those who love him' (1 Cor. 2:9).

It does us well to remember that Eden is a type, or representation of the Garden of Heaven. All that Eden was, Heaven is and more! Heaven is the eternal Garden of God. The place of His dwelling, the place where He walks and talks with His children, all those who have come home from their wanderings. It is the place where He abundantly provides "more than we can ask or think." It is in Heaven that the full measure of all that God intended for His prize creation is fulfilled. It is here that we "shall see Him as He is" and it is here that "we shall be like Him."

When we pass through the Garden of Gethsemane, when we surrender our way to His way, when we join our spirit, our heart, our mind, our very being with Christ there in the Garden of Pressing, our wants and desires all change. All we want, all we desire is Jesus.

If we have truly surrendered our will to His will, we long for Him to call us by name. This is the sacred romance of the Song of Songs that calls us homeward. This is the remembrance that stirs in the depths of our being and reminds us that our Father has more than enough. That our Father has a house with room for all His children. And he beckons us home.

He calls us by name to come home. "There have been times", says C. S. Lewis, "when I think we do not desire heaven but more often I find myself wondering whether, in our heart of hearts, we have ever desired anything else" (C. S. Lewis, *The Problem of Pain* New York: Macmillan, 1962, p. 145). With great longing, St. Paul speaks of being absent from the body as being present with Christ. That is Heaven. As the Catechism says:

> This perfect life with the Most Holy Trinity—this communion of life and love with the Trinity, with the Virgin Mary, the angels and all the blessed—is called "heaven." Heaven is the ultimate end and fulfillment of the deepest human longings, the state of supreme, definitive happiness. (CCC 1024)

It is Heaven and we see God 'face to face." It is Heaven and He calls us by name (see Rev. 2:17). It is Heaven and we join the saints, great and small, and the angels as the friends of God! In blessed communion! Gathered around the throne of God. The throne that from under flows a river! It is the river of the water of life! (Rev. 22). All who are thirsty can drink freely of it. (Remember the river that flowed out of Eden and watered the earth? Or the woman at the well who longed for the water that Jesus promised? The water that would slake thirst forever? Come and drink freely!) And better still, the Tree of Life is on either side of the river. (Don't ask me how!) Healing is in its leaves. The Tree of Calvary bringing for its eternal fruit! The marriage feast of the Lamb, complete and full for all the faithful!

And God will be our God and we shall be His people. His name shall be on our foreheads, not as the mark of a beast, not as the mark of ownership, but as the mark of family, as the mark of His people. Eden will be recapitulated, but no longer as a shadow of that which is to come, but as the fulness of the presence and glory of God. Shared with His people.

The beatific vision as we behold Him face to face. That is Heaven. As we enter into and share in His blessed life forever and ever more!

The Garden of Paradise, the completed Garden of Eden. Eden was, after all, paradise on earth. The abundance, the provision, the peace. All were part of Eden, and all are part of Heaven. Isaiah says that the wolf and the lamb, the leopard, and the young goats will be at peace, and even a child will lead them. Isaiah also describes Heaven by saying that:

> On this mountain the LORD of hosts will make for all peoples a feast of fat things, a feast of choice wines—of fat things full of marrow, of choice wines well refined. And he will destroy on this mountain the covering that is cast over all peoples, the veil that is spread over all nations. He will swallow up death for ever, and the Lord GOD will wipe away tears from all faces, and the reproach of his people he will take away from all the earth, for the LORD has spoken. (Isa. 25:6- 8)

Sounds like what we read in the Book of Revelation! God is preparing a feast for His people. He is, if you will, preparing the fatted calf for that great "Welcome Home" banquet.

Like the Father in the parable of the Prodigal, He welcomes us with a holy kiss and says, "Enter into your reward." The New Jerusalem, the new Holy Mountain of God. So, press on! Join St. Paul as he says to run the race to win the prize! Agonize in the Garden of Gethsemane and surrender as often as you must. Walk through the Garden of Resurrection and hear the Master Gardener call you by name. Sit at His feet in communion and learn of His ways. But press on! Keep walking with Him. Heaven is just in sight.

Epilogue

It's Suppertime

Come home, come home! It's suppertime! (Ira Stanphill)

The kids in the neighborhood where I grew up would often play together in the evening. We would play baseball or football in the street in front of our homes. Sometimes we would play hide and seek. Other times we just played catch together.

When Mother had supper on the table, we would hear the voice of our father calling us to come home. Our names would ring out. Each one of us was called to come home. There was nothing quite like the certainty of hearing that name ring out. There was nothing quite like walking into the house and being greeted by the aroma of a freshly cooked meal! Knowing we each had a place at the table. We belonged here. Our father made it so. While not extravagant, there was always enough.

Can you hear the Father calling? Can you get just a taste of glory divine? This longing for home, the home that God intended. The home that God created. The home that God inhabits. Jesus says, "in my Father's house are many rooms (mansions), I go to prepare you a place!" That is heaven. That is ultimate, lasting, joyful fulfillment. To be home, to be in heaven. Heaven simply is the Kingdom of God, where God is, is heaven. Without God, it is hell. I am ready! How about you? Let's go Home! It's almost suppertime! It's almost time to behold Him face to face. It's almost time to enjoy communion with our Father, the Creator of All, forever. It's almost time to go home.

ABOUT THE AUTHOR

Carl Floyd is a former Protestant minister who has converted to the Catholic faith. He was ordained in 1978 as an Assemblies of God minister. In addition to pastoring churches large and small, Carl has been the voice of commercials for Delta Airlines, National Geographic, Kentucky Fried Chicken, Village Inn, and more! In 2015 Carl converted to Catholicism at the Easter Vigil in 2015. In 2019 he completed a Master of Arts degree in theology at the Augustine Institute. Carl is an instituted acolyte and fully certified catechist in the Archdiocese of Galveston Houston. He served as a Pastoral Associate at Immaculate Conception Catholic Church in Sealy, TX. where he was responsible for Faith Formation. Carl has presented parish missions and retreats. Carl serves on the Board of Directors for the Sealy Pregnancy Resource Center. Carl and his wife, Dr. Cathy Floyd reside in Texas with their three dogs!

Look for his upcoming book *"How to Get Ahead in the World (that is to come): Leading Your Children in What Really Matters"*

Made in the USA
Columbia, SC
02 March 2025

54593646R00093